ACK

0750 933 682 0 158 X4

D0548038

Roaring Boys

Playwrights and Players in Elizabethan
and Jacobean England

JUDITH COOK

Foreword by Gregory Doran

SUTTON PUBLISHING

First published in 2004 by
Sutton Publishing Limited
Phoenix Mill · Thrupp · Stroud
Gloucestershire · GL5 2BU

British Library Cataloguing in Publication Data
A catalogue record for this book is available from the British
Library.

ISBN 0-7509-3368-2

Typeset in 11/14.5pt Sabon.
Typesetting and origination by
Sutton Publishing Limited.
Printed and bound in England by
J.H. Haynes & Co. Ltd, Sparkford.

Contents

List of Illustrations

Foreword

I'm in the middle of putting together a season of plays by Shakespeare's contemporaries to celebrate the twentieth season of the Swan Theatre in Stratford-upon-Avon. The Swan was built to stage the plays that had inspired Shakespeare and that he inspired: a huge canon of little-known works. So when Trevor Nunn was preparing to open the Swan, he and Judith Cook thought up the notion of producing an introduction to these neglected playwrights, which appeared as *At the Sign of the Swan* in 1986. Imagine my delight, then, when I received a letter from Judith asking me to write a foreword to her latest book on the subject.

Royal Shakespeare Company audiences are now more familiar with the plays that were performed alongside the works of Shakespeare at the Rose, the Globe and Blackfriars. In 2002 I produced a season of rare Jacobean plays, which went on to enjoy an unprecedented run in London's West End, testifying to a vigorously healthy renewed appetite for this repertoire.

Since the Swan opened, we have done most of the major comedies of Ben Jonson, virtually all the plays of Christopher Marlowe, the famous Websters, alongside Marston, Massinger, Middleton, with Ford and Fletcher, and even Shirley and Shadwell. But there are huge gaps – some of the Roaring Boys in this book have hardly had a look-in: very little Dekker, no George Peele yet, and no Robert Greene.

We may know the plays a little more. Judith Cook introduces us to the characters who wrote them. And now I feel responsible. For having read Judith's excellent survey of the period, and having been introduced to the likes of Robert Greene, in his doublet of goose-turd green, with his wild hair, pointed red beard, and his punk,

v

Emma, sister to Cutting Ball Jack, I feel I ought to honour the acquaintance and put on his plays immediately.

Roaring Boys chronicles those dangerous decades at the end of the sixteenth and start of the seventeenth centuries when British Theatre exploded into being. Judith Cook presents its *dramatis personae* – Henslowe's madcap stable of writers. She paints a vivid picture of the theatres for which they were writing, of the audience to whom they performed, and of the police state that controlled them. Her meticulous attention to detail is delightful, and her insights into the role of women, for example, the impact of asylum seekers and regime change in that society, are both revealing and resonant.

I was away on tour in Japan when Judith's letter arrived. When I got back I accepted her invitation, only to receive an e-mail by return from her son Nick, telling me the sad news of her sudden death. I am sorry I never met her. But her book testifies to her enthusiasm for her subject, her encyclopedic knowledge of the period, and her rare gift for storytelling.

Gregory Doran
Stratford-upon-Avon, 2004

Acknowledgements

I would like to thank the helpful staff of the British Library, Bodleian Library, Corpus Christi College, Cambridge, the Courtauld Institute, Dulwich College, Dulwich Picture Gallery, National Portrait Gallery and Shakespeare Birthplace Trust Library for their assistance, and Walter Hodges for allowing me to use his drawing of the Rose Theatre. Also Jaqueline Mitchell for her help and encouragement.

Judith Cook
Newlyn, Cornwall, 2003

Prologue

The scene: a busy early afternoon sometime in October 1591. The place: the Bankside, its gambling dens, brothels, ordinaries (the Elizabethan equivalent of fast food cafés), taverns, the Clink prison (one of five gaols in Southwark), the Bear Pit and the Rose Theatre, built by the businessman and entrepreneur Philip Henslowe four years earlier and now, after several months of closure, reopened, enlarged and improved.

The cast: the people of London, the merchants, cheapjacks, cutpurses and whores (the latter known as 'Winchester Geese'), the young bloods on the make, the merry wives (some seeking assignations), the bands of apprentice boys out looking for trouble, the hundreds of ordinary folk who have come to see a performance at the Rose of the most popular play of the day, *The Spanish Tragedy* by Thomas Kyd. Both before and after they cross the Thames they are at risk, as they battle through the capital's congested streets, of being run down by the increasingly heavy traffic. As John Stow grumbles: 'The world now runs on wheels with many whose parents were glad to go on foot.'

Further along the Bankside and going in the opposite direction, his feet squeezed into fashionable boots, is one of the theatrical world's prime self-publicists, the poet and playwright Robert Greene. His wine-stained doublet is in his favourite colour, 'goose turd', a virulent yellowy-green. His red hair is greased into a cone shape behind his head while his beard, according to fellow-poet and wit, Thomas Nashe, 'is long and red like a steeple, which he cherished continually without cutting, whereat he might hang a jewel, it is so sharp and pendant'. Behind him trudges his mistress, Emma Ball, who has recently discovered that she is pregnant. Her brother is the notorious highwayman Cutting Ball Jack. Several people stop Greene to ask whether he is intending to see *The Spanish Tragedy* that afternoon, but Greene tells them in an offhand way that he has better things to do with his time.

The real reason is that he dare not show his face at the Rose after having palmed off on to Henslowe and the company of the Lord Admiral's Men his play *Orlando Furioso*, assuring them it was a completely new work, for which Henslowe had paid him the substantial sum of twenty nobles – only to discover, after it had been rehearsed and given a public performance, that he had already sold the same script to the Lord Pembroke's Men who were now touring it around the country.

Meanwhile in the lodgings he shares with Kyd when he is in town, Christopher Marlowe is working on his own new play, *Edward II*. Currently there is a vogue for historical epics following the success of *Henry VI* (in which he had had a hand), and *Richard III*, the tale of Crookbacked Dick written by the newcomer from Stratford-upon-Avon and a play which is rapidly catching up with *The Spanish Tragedy* in terms of popularity. Not that Marlowe need worry; his very first offering, *Tamburlaine*, was a smash hit – making him an instant celebrity. However, hardly anyone who will sit, or more likely stand, to see the first performance of *Edward II* will have any idea what they will be in for. They will soon learn. Marlowe reads over the lines he has given Edward when he tells his favourite and lover, Piers Gaveston, the nature of the entertainment he is proposing for him:

> Sometime a lovely boy in Dian's shape,
> With hair that gilds the water as it glides,
> Crownets of pearl about his naked arms,
> And in his sportful hands an olive-tree,
> To hide those parts which men delight to see . . .

Kit Marlowe, the first of the gay Cambridge spies, is giving the world his own take on the subject of kingship.

Prologue

The later years of the reign of Queen Elizabeth I ushered in what can only be described as the explosion of a new art form: that of professional drama – and professional drama required professional writers. What follows are the stories of some of those hopeful young men, often from very ordinary backgrounds, who were to find themselves caught up in the excitement, fame and dangers of the London theatre scene.

INTRODUCTION

Dangerous Times – the New World of Theatre

> Six days after these were burned to death
> God sent us our Elizabeth.
> Note in *The Register* (11 November 1558)

If your ambition was to become a celebrated and popular dramatist or a famous and acclaimed actor, then you could not have chosen a better time to be born than the middle or late sixteenth century. No need for Arts Councils, subsidies or writers-in-residence; the theatrical world, desperate to service the new and growing entertainment scene and its huge audiences, was crying out for you and your work. As with Hollywood in the 1930s, the London theatre scene, run by the early entrepreneurs such as Philip Henslowe, sucked in talented writers not only from within the capital (which might be expected), but also from the provinces. A few of the new writers were born into comparative wealth, but far more, including Shakespeare, belonged to the first generation of the sons of artisans to have acquired a secondary education in the new grammar schools.

What might be called the golden age of English theatre lasted roughly from the building of the first proper playhouse in 1576 to about 1620, and there is no doubt that the Queen's accession in 1558 ushered in an extraordinary era in which the arts could flourish. But before opening a door into the world of the theatre, it might be useful first to have a brief look at what was happening outside in the real world, for there was a dichotomy running through almost every aspect of life and society. Great creativity burgeoned alongside almost routine brutality, awesome magnificence next to appalling squalor, a thirst for new knowledge

1

set against shocking ignorance. Beneath the surface of the Merry England of myth there lurked always the dark, dangerous world of political intrigue, treason, danger and death.

Professional theatre came into being at a time when men were still getting to grips with the idea that the world was round and that it circled round the sun, not the sun round the earth. There was the excitement of the new sciences, of astronomy and mathematics. Secretly and behind closed doors, people were actually questioning the truth of the stories told in the Old Testament, even such matters as how long it really was between the Creation and the present day. We know that such discussions went on because Marlowe attended one such group, often known as the 'School of the Night', where questions were asked such as how it could possibly have taken so long for the Jews to reach the promised land, though Marlowe took his criticism of the scriptures further, much further.[1] But even while the more sophisticated citizenry were considering such matters, conventional religious belief was still virtually universal. Almost everyone believed that there really was a heaven and a hell, that at the end of your life you had to account directly to God for your misdeeds, and that there would be a Judgement Day when the graves gave up their dead. Most people also believed in witches and witchcraft, not to mention fairies.

The extraordinary renaissance had come about in no small part because of the circumstances surrounding the Queen's accession. She came to the throne to the acclaim of a fearful and demoralised population which had been exposed for the previous six years to the fires of Smithfield and elsewhere, death at the stake being the punishment meted out to heretics on the authority of a woman totally convinced of the rightness of her actions, a woman who had compounded her unpopularity by taking as her husband King Philip II of Spain. Now Mary Tudor, 'Bloody Mary', was dead and the country breathed again. The two lines of verse by an anonymous writer at the beginning of the chapter express the overwhelming feeling of relief.

One of the statements made by Elizabeth at the start of her reign was that she had no desire to seek 'windows into men's souls'.

Although the church had reverted again to Protestantism and she, like her father, was its defender, she did not want to rule over a country riven by religious tensions. Therefore Catholics who behaved themselves and were loyal to the crown were left alone, so long as they paid their fines for missing church of a Sunday. It was a fine aspiration to which, in the early days, the government on the orders of the Queen did its best to adhere, though as time went by dangers, both internally and from Europe, would combine to prevent its continuance.

Elizabeth's Court was splendid. From the first she dressed magnificently, decked with jewels, her face framed in the finest of lace ruffs, gowned in enormous farthingales covered in beadwork, seed pearls and embroidery. She employed tried and trusted advisers such as William Cecil, Lord Burleigh, who had stood by her throughout some of the worst times of her life, and Sir Francis Walsingham, Secretary of State to the Privy Council. She surrounded herself with the most handsome courtiers, the prettiest young women and the best artists, musicians and poets of the day. When she went on one of her great progresses around the country, people turned out in their hundreds simply to watch her pass. She was, indeed, Gloriana. Her Court again offers two sides of the coin. Among the favoured poets of the era were Edmund Spenser and Walter Ralegh. Spenser might well laud Elizabeth in *The Faerie Queen* and Ralegh turn a pretty sonnet when he was not throwing his cloak down for the Queen to tread on, but both were involved in the most appalling acts of violence in Ireland, Ralegh joining in a massacre at which not only unarmed men were put to the sword but where women and children were also slaughtered. Renaissance Man indeed had many facets, but unthinking violence is rarely mentioned among them.

Outside the Court in the City, the hub of commerce, visitors from overseas marvelled at the wealth of the merchants in their great mansions, the shopkeepers and tradesmen of every kind, the thriving markets. England's great merchant venturers sailed their argosies to every corner of the known world bringing back with them, to City harbours like Billingsgate, exotic cargoes of silks, spices and ivory along with tales of strange people in stranger lands. Outside, in the country, the nobles and the wealthy built themselves grandiose stately homes which they decked with tapestries and furnished with fine furniture. To complete the picture, common land was enclosed to make their parks and great, formal gardens. Yet around the walls of the City of London itself huddled the shanty towns of the poor and those who had trudged up from the provinces to seek their fortune, clusters of dwellings in what we might describe now as 'no-go areas', looked on by honest citizens as nothing more than cauldrons of disease and crime. The picture Elizabeth offered to the people of England, and indeed to the world outside, was one of immense confidence, conspicuous consumption, success at home and abroad and the feeling that the English were indeed living in a golden age. But underneath it all that dark, disturbing and dangerous world remained, only a hair's breadth away.

From the first the Queen had been well aware of the dangers besetting her. All those endless negotiations over marriages which she never had any intention of going through with, the delicate and secret embassies to Europe, the stately dances of diplomacy, were designed with only one end in mind: to keep the Queen on the throne and the country safe from foreign invaders. The obvious threats were from Spain and France but there was also danger much nearer home. In 1560, two years after Elizabeth's accession to the English throne, King Francis II of France died and the following year his widow, the young Mary, Queen of Scots, returned home. Unsurprisingly, given her charm, looks, position and lack of judgement, she soon became a honeypot for ambitious men wanting to marry her and get their hands on the levers of power. She chose disastrously, marrying her cousin, Lord Darnley, in 1565. Within three years she had given birth to the heir to the Scottish throne, had very possibly been complicit in the murder of her husband, had scandalised her government by involving herself with the Earl of Bothwell and, after arrest and imprisonment, had escaped to England seeking sanctuary.

Despite the long history of enmity with Scotland, Elizabeth reluctantly agreed to her plea with the result that from that day until her death over twenty years later, Mary was the ready-made figurehead with a claim to the English throne around which malcontents and Catholic plotters could gather. Indeed, within a year of her arrival the Catholic Earls of Northumberland and Westmorland were planning rebellion, while the Catholic Earl of Norfolk, Thomas Percy, was making overtures of marriage to her, which she was encouraging for all she was worth. Popular romance has Mary as a martyred heroine, taking little or no part in the activities undertaken in her name, but she was soon sending messages to the Spanish Duke of Alva asking for help for the Earls. 'Tell your master', she wrote to him, 'that if he will help me, I shall be Queen of England in three months.' No doubt about that then.

The Privy Council got wind of what was afoot and Norfolk was sent for and shrewdly advised to be honest with the Queen. Later, as he faced execution, he wished he had been. Instead, what followed was the abortive Northern Rebellion which was put down with great savagery, some eight hundred of the Earl's followers being hanged. Northumberland fled to Scotland but was later returned to England and executed. Elizabeth refused to act against Mary on the grounds that there was no certain proof that she had been party to the plot, but so major an insurrection thoroughly unnerved both the Queen and her government, and matters were soon to deteriorate further. In February 1570 Pope Pius V issued his notorious Bull of Excommunication against the Queen, the result of which was to make it almost impossible for her government to separate faith from politics as had hitherto been the case. The Pope had put English Catholics in an impossible position: if they remained loyal to the Queen they were disobedient to the commands of the Holy Father in Rome, yet if they obeyed his edict it followed that they were traitors to the Queen. The Bull made the position quite clear: all the subjects of the English realm were freed from their oaths of allegiance 'and all manner of duty, fidelity and obedience'. But even that was not enough. The Pope 'commanded and enjoined all and every subject and people whatsoever that they shall not once dare to obey her or her laws, directions or commands, binding under the same curse those who do anything to the contrary'. In other words those remaining loyal to the Crown faced automatic excommunication. More than that, it was now open season for assassins.

In 1572 the Ridolfi Plot led finally to the execution of the Earl of Norfolk, a deed accompanied by a demand from Parliament for Mary's head. Again Elizabeth refused. Then in August, while she was staying at Warwick Castle, the news was brought to her of the horrific massacre of Huguenots which had taken place on St Bartholomew's Eve, first in Paris then spreading out to other towns and cities, bringing with it an influx of asylum seekers into England. By the 1580s storm clouds were gathering from every direction. In 1583 there were two more plots, those of Somerville and Throgmorton, both designed to pave the way for a Spanish invasion. That both failed was due in no small part to the intelligence-gathering skills of Sir Francis Walsingham's agents. Then, in 1586, intelligence reached the Queen's spymaster of yet another, the initiator being a naive country gentleman by the name of Antony Babington. The government had had enough and were absolutely determined that Mary should go. To ensure this she had to be implicated beyond any shadow of doubt; Walsingham therefore infiltrated into the circle of the conspirators his own best secret agent, Robert Poley. The result, as everyone knows, was not only the downfall and unpleasant deaths of the plotters but the eventual execution of Mary, Queen of Scots.

But no sooner had one hazard been put behind her than the Queen was beset by others. Although 'the Spanish Armada' of 1588 is usually referred to as the single attempt by Philip II to conquer the English, Spain had actually prepared for an invasion the previous year, not with flotillas of galleons but by vessels towing barges full of soldiers over from the Low Countries; and it might well have succeeded had it not been for the English raid on Cadiz which destroyed some of the fleet. The real Spanish Armada was a far more hazardous venture for the Spaniards than the first would have been and was soundly defeated by a combination of superior English seamanship in more manoeuvrable ships and the appalling weather. Her leadership of the country during that time and the vanquishing of the Armada was Elizabeth's finest hour, her speech at Tilbury worthy of Shakespeare. But Spain's determination to invade did not end there; there were at least two other abortive attempts afterwards, with Ireland being used as a base. No one can pretend that what England did in Ireland during the last half of the sixteenth century was anything of which to be proud, but it should also be remembered that the government considered their western neighbour to be their Achilles' heel.

The great flowering of the dramatists in the 1590s was therefore accompanied by increasing paranoia on the part of the government, the implementation of draconian laws against Catholic 'Mass priests', along with other repressive legislation to deal with civil unrest. In 1593 the latter would catch in its net both Thomas Kyd and Christopher Marlowe, at the scene of whose murder we come across once again that very same Robert Poley who played such a vital role in the bringing to justice of the Babington plotters. From then until the Queen's death in 1603, there was war in Ireland, continuing uncertainty as to the succession since Elizabeth refused to name King James of Scotland as her heir, and the abortive final plot, that of the Queen's last great favourite, the inept Earl of Essex, whose arrogance finally brought him to the block. Nor did the death of the Queen and the subsequent coronation of James VI of Scotland as James I of England make the profession of dramatist any less hazardous. Anti-Catholic feeling became even more ferocious, factionalism even more intense at Court where the King was swayed by a succession of favourites. It was an age in which almost anything could be bought.

Throughout it all, mostly unaware, or uncaring, of the affairs of state (with the exception of the threat from the Armada), the people of London packed the playhouses. The times might be dangerous but the people were well able to live with that. Death was ever present and, in Marlowe's words, they lived 'on the slicing edge' of it: death from disease, particularly from the regular epidemics of plague, death at the hands of a robber in the street, or following a quarrel at a time when insults led easily to fights and men routinely wore swords and daggers, while for women there was always the very real fear of death in childbirth or the dreaded puerperal fever associated with it.

Their idea of entertainment, however, was a broad one. The very same audiences which crowded into the Rose and the Globe to laugh at *The Shoemaker's Holiday* or enjoy the poetry of *Twelfth Night* were equally happy to visit the Bear Pit the following day or stand at the front of the crowd at Tyburn to watch the public hangings. But theatre opened up for them whole new worlds: those of kingship and its power and responsibilities in the great historical epics, of hubris followed by nemesis as portrayed in the characters of Marlowe's great over-reachers, of betrayal and murder set alongside the foibles of humanity in the great tragedies and comedies of Shakespeare – not to mention the nature of love.

ONE

The New Professionals

A play's a true transparent crystal mirror,
To show good minds their mirth, the bad their terror.
                    Thomas Heywood, *Apology for Actors* (1612)

By the time Heywood wrote these words a visitor to London could have joined audiences at eight or nine playhouses and even if, as was likely, not all of them were open for business at the same time, he or she might well have had the choice of anything up to a dozen plays from which to choose within the space of a week. Hundreds, indeed thousands, of people might pack into any one performance at a large theatre such as the Globe when it was full to capacity, a good many of them, of course, standing for the privilege. Shrewd actors such as Edward Alleyn and playwrights like William Shakespeare had become very wealthy men; there was money to be made in the theatre for both actors and writers even if all too many of them let it slip through their fingers and drank or gambled it away. The actor Richard Burbage was just as much a star to the audiences of his day as Sir Laurence Olivier or Sir Ian McKellen four hundred years later.

However, by then theatre had become properly established. It was nothing like as easy for the pioneers of a quarter of a century earlier; indeed it would have been almost impossible for them to imagine what the future might hold. Companies of players did not, of course, suddenly appear from nowhere once playhouses started being built. Plays had been regularly, if seasonally, performed since early medieval times by the various guilds, and cycles of religious dramas such as those of the York, Wakefield, Coventry and Chester Mysteries and the Cornish 'Ordinalia' were popular and provided a

9

welcome break in the working year. No doubt some of those craftsmen taking part were talented actors but they were quite definitely amateurs. At major festivals such as Christmas or May Day there was lighter fare like the Mummers' plays which might well incorporate, along with their regular characters, those of Robin Hood and Maid Marian. Noblemen and other wealthy landowners would also keep among their servants those able to perform 'interludes' for the entertainment of guests, though these were hardly theatrical performances as we understand them and often took place while everyone was eating, drinking and chatting.

Gradually the repertoire grew, first with the appearance of the morality plays, of which the best known example is *Everyman*, though still as the name suggests with a religious theme; then, mainly for private consumption within schools and colleges, broader and more adventurous drama. In 1534, when Henry VIII was still on the throne, Nicholas Udall became headmaster of Eton College. He had a keen interest in drama and wrote a number of plays for the boys, one of which, *Ralph Roister Doister*, still survives. It was immensely popular and there are references to it being performed years later. Its comic theme was to influence a whole generation of professional playwrights, for the main character, Doister himself, is a swaggering, roistering, woman-chasing, cowardly buffoon with a high opinion of himself, who gets his come-uppance at the hands of a determined lady. Doister is a likely prototype for the Falstaff of *The Merry Wives of Windsor*.

By the time Elizabeth came to the throne, bands of players along with tumblers and musicians were travelling around the countryside playing in the towns and villages, especially at fairs and on public holidays, offering drama which was pure entertainment. The general population loved the arrival of the players and flocked to see the plays but their betters took a very different view of the matter. Players were considered no better than the 'sturdie beggars', tinkers, vagabonds, thieves and masterless men who roamed the countryside in bands. As to what they performed, plays were 'the Devil's sermons' and those who performed them should be whipped out of town with the other travelling scum. Such was the prejudice that actors realised drastic action was needed if they were to survive, and it was fortunate that the growing wealth and ostentation of the aristocracy was set to provide it. Actors were suddenly in demand as it became the fashion for a lord or earl to have his own company of players as part of the household. Their patrons' desire to advertise their wealth and success thus enabled the actors to perform legally and without fear of the consequences, so long as they were officially known by the name of their patron as, for example, the Earl of Leicester's Men.[1]

Under the auspices of a powerful patron, players were able to continue touring so long as they were available to perform for him whenever they were required to do so, and we know of a number of inns and taverns, particularly in London, regularly visited by acting companies 'where money is paid or demanded for hearing plays'. In 1567 John Brayne, a grocer, and the brother-in-law of James Burbage (father of the famous Richard), paid out £8 10s for scaffolding for plays performed at the Red Lion in Stepney. 'James Burbage was a joiner', notes M.C. Bradbrook in *The Rise of the Common Player*, 'and knew all about scaffolding'. Another inn, the Bell, was so often used by players that they stored their costumes there, while the landlord set about acquiring stage props and properties which could be hired out to acting companies for a fee. Some inns became particularly associated with individual companies and we know that the Earl of Leicester's Men played regularly at the Cross Keys in Gracechurch Street.[2]

Faced with the growing number of actors' companies and in an attempt to gain some control of what was going on, in 1572 the government brought in the notorious Vagabonds Act, which lumped together all the various groups travelling around the countryside, however loosely organised. According to the Statute:

all Fencers, Bearwards, Common Players in Enterludes & Minstrels not belonging to any Baron of this Realme or towards any other honourable Personage of greater Degree; all Jugglers, Pedlars, Tinkers and Petty Chapmen, and have not Licence of two Justices of the Peace at the least, whereof one to be of the

Quorum when and in what Shire they shall happen to wander . . . shall be taken and adjudged to be deemed Rogues, Vagabonds and Sturdie Beggars.

It was, therefore, absolutely essential to have a patron, with the result that theatre flourished.

Two years later, as Bradbrook points out, in the March of 1574, it struck someone at Court that since whatever the prohibitions brought in and the dire punishments threatened, such entertainment now appeared to be here to stay, instead of continuing to put obstacles in its way, why not try and make some money out of it for the Exchequer?[3] How would it be if the government offered licences for places in which plays could legitimately be performed? That way money could be made in the form of a new tax, while an eye could also be kept on the content of the plays that were being put on. The Lord Chamberlain, therefore, wrote a civil letter to the Lord Mayor of London putting forward this excellent notion and requesting that it immediately be put into practice, only to be met by an outright refusal. The principal reason given for this was that the City Fathers, and they alone, had the power to restrict assembly and keep control of what went on in the City and such a power therefore could not be delegated to anyone else. However, when the situation was looked into further, it appeared that the City had already seen the money-making possibilities of such a scheme and were themselves busily collecting money from players 'for poor relief' by allowing them the privilege of playing within the city walls and that this was a practice they had no intention of giving up.

For a while, the Lord Chamberlain continued to negotiate, suggesting ways and means by which such poor relief could continue, but when the Lord Mayor remained adamant, he overruled his objections and the first Letters Patent were given to the Earl of Leicester's Men under the Great Seal of England on behalf of Her Majesty, Queen Elizabeth I. They were granted to James Burbage, John Perkyn, John Laneham, William Johnson and Robert Wilson:

to use, exercise, and occupy the art and faculty of playing comedies tragedies interludes stage plays and such other like as they have already used and studied or hereafter shall use and study as well for the recreation of your loving subjects as for our solace and pleasure . . . as also to use and occupy all such instruments as they have already practised . . . to shew publish exercise and occupy to their best commodity . . . as well within our City of London and liberties of the same, as also within the liberties and freedoms of any of our cities, towns and boroughs, etc. as without the same, any act statute proclamation or commandment to the contrary not withstanding, provided the said comedies tragedies interludes and stage plays be by the Master of our Revels (for the time being) before seen and allowed and that the same be not published or shewen [*sic*] in the time of common prayer or in the time of great and common plague in our said City of London.

It was the first ever official recognition by the establishment of theatre as we know and understand it today and it remains unique. The Letters Patent overrode the ancient rights of the city to determine what took place within its boundaries in the face of dire warnings from the objectors as to the horrors about to be unleashed on an unsuspecting public. There would be, without doubt

the inordinate haunting of great multitudes of people, especially youth, to plays, interludes and shows, leading to affrays, quarrels, and evil practices of incontinency in great Inns, having chambers and secret places adjoining to their open stages and galleries, thus inveigling and alluring maids, especially orphans and good Citizens' children [who are] under age, to privy and unmeet shows, the publishing of unchaste, uncomely and unashamed fast speeches and doings and the withdrawing of Her Majesty's subjects from divine service and holy days.

Not only that, such entertainments would lead to the 'unthrifty waste of money by the poor, sundry robberies by pickpockets and cutpurses, the uttering of popular, busy and seditious matters and many other corruptions of youth and other enormities', not to mention the possible 'slaughters and mayhems of the Queen's subjects by falling scaffolding, breaking frames and stages and the use of gunpowder'.[4]

The Earl of Leicester's Men had therefore achieved their aim of official recognition not only for themselves but on behalf of other such companies. Thus emboldened, on 13 May 1576 James Burbage signed a 21-year lease on a building plot in Holywell on the public road between Shoreditch and Bishopsgate not far from Finsbury Fields and at once set about building the first custom-built playhouse. He called it simply The Theatre. His lease contained a clause which said that if he spent £200 or more on the building, he could take it down when the lease expired. He was also supposed to be offered an automatic extension of the lease if he wanted it, although the terms would have to be renegotiated. Within a year The Theatre was joined by a second playhouse, The Curtain, close by. The memory of The Curtain, which remained in use for over thirty years, still lingers on in 'Curtain Road' which runs between Old Street and Great Eastern Street. We do not know who built The Curtain but it has been suggested that it was a syndicate of actors and that the two playhouses complemented each other, possibly sharing wardrobe and other storage facilities.

We have no description or sketches of what they were like but theatre historian Andrew Gurr considers it likely that The Theatre was closely based on the design of the rectangular and galleried inn yards in which Burbage and the Earl of Leicester's company usually played, while The Curtain was more like the 'wooden O' familiar from prints of the later Bankside theatres.[5] However, unless the foundations of one or the other are discovered during building excavations, as happened with the Rose Theatre in Southwark, we are unlikely ever to know. Although all authorities give The Theatre as the first proper playhouse, other excavations have revealed that there is a possibility that there was an earlier one, the Red Lion in Whitechapel built by John Brayne in about 1567; if this were the case it was not built specifically for the performance of plays but mainly for bear-baiting. While The Theatre and The Curtain were primarily for the production of plays, the stages were also used for a wide variety of other events such as exhibitions of sword-fighting, wrestling, tumbling, vaulting, something referred to as 'rope dancing', and possibly, on occasion, even bear-baiting, although that is by no means certain. Even after the building of the two theatres, acting companies continued to give performances regularly in the yards of inns such as the Bell, the Cross Keys and the Bull to the north of the City, the Belsavage in the west and the George in Southwark.

Nevertheless the City Fathers remained unhappy at the close proximity of the two theatres to their boundaries and rarely missed an opportunity to cancel performances or even close them down for weeks at a time at the slightest excuse.

While Burbage's company played mainly at The Theatre it seems they also played at The Curtain from time to time, although the latter is more closely associated with Philip Henslowe. However, in 1587, with no end in sight to the constant battle between the City authorities and the two theatres, Philip Henslowe turned his attention to the Bankside, an area which had much to commend it as it was well outside the jurisdiction of the City, with easy access either by London Bridge or by the host of boats, up to three thousand of them, plying for trade across and up and down the Thames. There were gardens alongside the river and there were several bear pits, drawing in plenty of trade, for those who also liked bear-baiting. Henslowe might well have commissioned great drama and employed amazingly talented actors, but he was above all a businessman and the Bankside also offered entertainments of a more robust nature: it was notorious for its gaming houses, brothels and low life. Another plus was that he already had his timber warehouse on that side of the Thames and either then, or shortly afterwards, he bought a house on the Bankside, along with a bear pit next door to it.

So, close to the old London Bridge with its houses and shops, Henslowe built one of the two most famous early playhouses, the Rose. Until relatively recently it was thought that the Rose was not built until 1592 but new research, following the discovery of its foundations in 1989, suggests that it opened in 1587 and was extended and improved five years later. In 1596 Francis Langley built another theatre on the Bankside, the Swan, and it is because of the drawings of it made that year by Johannes de Witt that we know something of what the Elizabethan playhouses looked like inside, although some of the details in the drawings do not fit what is now known about the interior of such theatres. However, the overall plan was right. Facing the audience as they entered a playhouse was the very large and high thrust stage, at the back of which was a gallery, area and 'discovery space' which could be concealed with a curtain. The stage itself was covered by a thatched roof supported on pillars and up above everything was a top storey, 'the hut', in which stage technicians worked and from which a trumpeter announced that a play would be performed that day. Three tiers of sheltered galleries ran round the walls; the big open space in front of the stage open to the elements, 'the pit', was for those standing to see the show.

In spite of the new playhouses, to keep within the law, acting companies still required patrons even if they were no longer attached to their households; among these were the Earls of Pembroke, Warwick, Derby, Essex, Worcester, Sussex, and Lord Strange. The two most prestigious noblemen to give their names to such companies were undoubtedly the Lord Admiral and the Lord Chamberlain, although it must be pointed out that patronage did not provide financial security; they were not subsidised in any way by those under whose name they performed. Such official recognition did, however, give the companies real status, bringing with it regular invitations to appear at Court.

Both companies were led by actors of exceptional ability in Edward Alleyn and Richard Burbage. The Lord Admiral's Men were particularly associated with Henslowe and the Rose Theatre, the Lord Chamberlain's Men with Burbage, first at The Theatre, then at the Globe. The companies were made up entirely of 'Men' because it was illegal for women to act on a public stage even if the ladies of the nobility regularly appeared at Court in interludes and masques, sometimes sporting costumes which elsewhere would have outraged public decency.

They worked on a sharer's system. Anything from half a dozen to a dozen of the most prominent people involved would put up a set sum of money, 'a share', in a particular company and theatre. Such sharers would include entrepreneurs such as Philip Henslowe, whose *Diaries* are one of our greatest sources of information on Elizabethan theatre, any financial backers, several of the leading actors in each company, and very possibly the wardrobe and props masters and the 'Bookman' or 'Book-keeper' who was in charge of all the scripts, ensuring that they did not fall into the wrong hands, as well as seeing to the copying out of 'the roles'. On occasion even a playwright could become a sharer as we know because William Shakespeare was one. Ben Jonson sought to emulate him, borrowing money from Henslowe to buy a share in the Lord Admiral's Men, although he gave it back fairly rapidly. Jonson's continual indebtedness to Henslowe is duly recorded in the *Diaries*.

The average acting company consisted of fifteen actors plus half a dozen apprentices. Apart from the sharers, the rest of the actors were 'hired men', taken on for anything from a single performance to a whole season, and it is likely that the companies also hired in people, to work backstage, assisting with stage effects and props as these became more elaborate, and helping with dressing and make-up. The young apprentices worked hard for their keep, doing all the running around, helping with effects such as working bellows for stage smoke, playing small parts like the devils who drag Faustus down to Hell and pages to noblemen and kings, before graduating to small speaking parts such as the fated princes in *Richard III*. Finally, the most talented had their 'three years to play' the women's roles.

Having a settled base in London did not prevent actors from going out on regular tours. Leading actors from, say, the Lord Admiral's Men would organise a tour with members of the Earl of Pembroke's Men or Lord Strange's Men, the temporary touring company travelling under one or other name. There were regular touring venues throughout the country such as Northampton, Coventry, Worcester, Gloucester, Shewsbury, Bristol and Exeter, but the companies would also set up and perform in the smaller towns en route. Tours took place for a variety of reasons: because a certain number of towns were used to having an annual visit from a theatre company and a loyal audience expected it; because audiences were thin on the ground in London; or when the authorities ordered the playhouses to close due either to public disorder or sickness. Not surprisingly, acting companies escaping from the plague in the plague years were quite likely to find themselves physically prevented from coming into a country town by citizens prepared to stone them out.

Leaving London for the provinces was always a chancy business and a good many tours proved to be financial disasters, one good example being that of a company led by Burbage, especially set up for a tour during the winter of 1592/3 (when plague closed the playhouses), which was so unsuccessful that its members had to sell everything, including all the costumes and props, leaving them with only what they stood up in. On another occasion Edward Alleyn, fearing a similar fate, sent home to his wife Joan (Henslowe's stepdaughter), via a kinsman who had called in to see the show, his best white waistcoat and other garments 'to be put safely away until his return'. Future correspondence, he told her, should be sent to him in Shrewsbury c/o Lord Strange's Men, which suggests, given how long it must have taken to send a letter, that the actors must have remained there for some time. Copies of correspondence between Edward and Joan Alleyn, when the former was on tour, are among Henslowe's papers and give a good idea of what exercised an actor who was away from home for weeks. Alleyn's pet name for Joan was 'Mouse':

'Mouse, you send me no news of anything,' he complains. 'You should send of your domestic matters, such things as happen at home, as how your distilled water proves this or that or any other thing you will . . . and, jug, I pray you let my orange tawny stockings of wool be dyed a good black against I come home to wear them in the winter. You send me no word of your garden but next time you will remember this, in any case, that all the bed which was parsley in the month of September, you should sow with spinach for then is the time. I would do so myself but we shall not come home 'til All Hallows tide, so farewell sweet Mouse.'

The letter was addressed to 'Mr. Hinslo on the Bankside, right over against the Clink'.[6]

Joan replied that she had seen to the dyeing of his stockings, had bought a good new bedstead and was busy planting out the spinach, but had been unable to buy the cloth he asked for as the plague had shut down the shops and the merchants. Nor had she been successful in selling his horse as he had also asked her to do. The best offer she had received was only £4 'so I have sent him into the country until your return'.

It also seems that English players did not confine themselves to touring in England. There are a number of somewhat scrappy reports of actors performing in Germany and of a company drawn from the Earl of Leicester's Men, which included Will Kempe, Thomas Pope and George Bryan, appearing in 1586 before the Danish Court in – where else – Elsinore. This writer was stunned to be told, when accompanying a theatre director to work in a theatre at Gdynia in Poland in the early 1990s, that there had long been a tradition in what is now Gdansk that Shakespeare's plays had been performed there before the end of the sixteenth century; a tradition possibly 'proved' a year or so later when the foundations of an Elizabethan-type playhouse were actually discovered there.

Those who had warned from the start that the building of the playhouses would lead to the end of all common decency, offering nothing but unlimited licence and immorality, soon considered their worst fears had been realised. In 1578, two years after the building of The Theatre, churchman John Stockwood thundered from the pulpit against the 'flocks of wild youths of both sexes, resorting to interludes, where both by lively gesture and voices there are allurements unto whoredom'.[7] Sour commentator Stephen Gosson, who left Oxford without obtaining his degree, confessed that while up at university he had himself tried his hand at writing plays 'but I burned one candle to seek another and lost both my time and my travail when I had done', and thus had learned his lesson. In the *School of Abuse* he writes that those who remain safely within the walls of academe, devoted to their love of learning and seeing 'but slender offences and small abuses' within their own walls, will never believe that there are 'such horrible monsters in playing places', for the actors, who are little better than beggars, 'jet under gentlemen's noses in suits of silk, exercising themselves to prating on the stage, and common scoffing when they come abroad, where they look askance over their shoulder at every man, of whom the Sunday before they begged alms'.[8] His warnings apparently unheeded and the theatres increasingly popular, a year later he described actors 'as the most dangerousest [*sic*] people in the world', no longer merely beggars but outright thieves and corrupters of the young, noting that the acting companies were now taking on apprentices to their trade and training them up 'to this abominable exercise'.

There was a general acceptance that London was overpopulated and filthy, with what amounted to open sewers running down the middle of the streets, not to mention the notoriously appalling state of the River Fleet, yet killjoys like Gosson and Stockwood were far more concerned by the 'filth' purveyed by the theatres than the raw sewage in the streets or the carcasses of dead animals floating down the Fleet. 'What availeth it to have sweet houses and stinking souls?' boomed Stockwood. God, he warned, would be noting the names of those who listened to the players rather than to preachers.

But such critics were whistling in the wind and there was one vital and missing ingredient from all that had gone before. With the ever-increasing popularity of the playhouses, the rapidly increasing professionalism of the theatre companies and the apparently insatiable demand for entertainment, there was, above all, a desperate need for plays of all kinds. Which is where the writers take centre stage, the lifestyles of many of whom would exceed the bigots' wildest nightmares. Enter the roaring boys.

TWO

The University Wits

... how many nets soever there be laid to take them, or hooks to choke them, they have ink in their bowels to darken the water; and sleights in their budgets to dry up the arm of every magistrate.

Stephen Gosson, *School of Abuse* (1582)

By the time the new professional playwrights were having their first works staged, London was already becoming a considerable tourist centre for the out-of-town visitor to see and marvel at. There were the lions at the Tower of London, the great church of St Paul's, packed with stallholders selling every kind of ware including souvenirs, the Bear Pit on the Bankside, not to mention London Bridge with its splendid shops and decaying heads on poles at its north end to give the onlooker a *frisson* of horror.

A young hopeful born and bred in London only had to walk into one of the playhouses and offer his services to Henslowe or Burbage, or collar a sharer in one of the companies and do his best to sell himself and his idea. For those from well out of town, from Devon, Norfolk or, indeed, Warwickshire, it would have been a considerable journey, made on horseback if they had sufficient funds, otherwise on foot, possibly augmented with lifts in carriers' carts – and without any certainty of success. Nor would they know their way around when they finally arrived and would need lodgings. Not surprisingly, in the early days these were mostly in the vicinity of The Theatre and The Curtain, in Shoreditch, Bishopsgate and Finsbury. No doubt some were soon parted from their money for the City teemed with those eager to part a fool (which is how most provincials were regarded) from his money, either by straight theft or more cunning ploys.

21

However, they were quick to learn and towards the end of the 1580s a newcomer to London, bent on visiting one of the playhouses and taking refreshment in a popular tavern before the afternoon's performance, might well find himself sitting in a corner quaffing his ale or sack watching a noisy group of young men sprawled around a table swapping jokes and anecdotes and making sure everyone present knew who they were. Indeed the author of the day's entertainment might well be among them and at least some would be members of the circle known as 'the University Wits'.

The earliest of these were 'the Oxford men' and included John Lyly, poet and playwright, George Peele, actor and playwright, Robert Greene, he of the pointed hair and beard and goose-turd green doublet, and the poets Thomas Watson, Thomas Lodge and Matthew Roydon. By the time we catch up with them in the late 1580s they had been joined by the poet and dramatist Christopher Marlowe, and the young, adder-tongued Thomas Nashe, poet and pamphleteer. There might also have been other playwrights and poets present, those who for various reasons never belonged to that particular magic circle. Among the outsiders was George Chapman, for not every 'Oxford man' sought to join the Wits, while Thomas Kyd and William Shakespeare left school without going on to college, spending their time earning a living by more practical means, Kyd as a professional 'scrivener' and Shakespeare working in his father's business. However, whatever their previous history might be, by 1590 Lyly, Peele, Greene, Marlowe, Chapman and Kyd were the leading figures in the first wave of professional dramatists, with Shakespeare coming up fast behind.

Professor Stanley Wells has referred to those young men in the London of the day as the 'roaring boys', describing them as the element of the 'anarchic and subversive' in the life of the period.[1] There are a number of references to roaring boys or 'roarers' in contemporary sources, an epithet used loosely to describe those given to noisy, showy and anti-social behaviour. 'I am Roughman', brags the character of that name in Thomas Heywood's *Fair Maid of the West* as he swaggers into a Cornish inn, catches sight of the pretty new barmaid and heroine of the tale and promptly clamps her to his chest, 'the only approved gallant of these parts and a man of whom the *roarers* stand in awe'.[2] Bess's spirited response to this is a slap on the face, followed a few days later by challenging him to a duel in the guise of a young man, a contest which she wins and to which she has invited an audience of locals who are hiding behind a convenient hedge to see the roarer get his come-uppance.

But 'roaring boys' as the element of the anarchic and subversive might equally well apply to the new breed of professional writers and their work, some of whom can only be described as arrant self-publicists, who would dominate the London theatre scene for the next forty years, drawn to the playhouses by the prospect of fame, fortune and, above all, opportunity. So who were they, where had they come from and how had they reached the point at which we meet them?

Apart from Nashe, they had all been born within the 10-year period from 1554 to 1564 and, given their widely differing circumstances, would have been unlikely ever to have known each other had it not been for the building of the playhouses. The eldest, John Lyly, 'a deft and dapper companion', cannot really be described as a roaring boy, for he was known for his courtesy and good behaviour. He was born in 1554 and we know very little about his origins except that he possibly went to the King's School in Cambridge and from there to Magdalen College, Oxford. As early as 1580 he was noted as having written 'light plays' for children's companies to be performed at Court. However, no one could describe George Peele, born in 1558, as being noted for good behaviour; in fact his name soon became a byword for riotous living and dissipation. His family had moved to London from Devonshire before his birth and his father was both a City Salter, a member of the Salters Guild, one of the great Livery Companies, and also Clerk to Christ's Hospital, a post which brought with it a rather fine property in which the family lived. Peele, therefore, was born into a comfortable background and because of his father's position and status was a 'free scholar' at Christ's Hospital before going on to Broadgates Hall, Oxford (now Pembroke College), taking his BA in 1577 and his MA in 1578. He was already becoming known for his verse and early attempts at drama while still at university.

Of Robert Greene we know a great deal more since he wrote copiously of his own life and times. He was born in Norwich about 1560 into what must have been a good family for, although he does not tell us what his father's trade or profession was, he writes that his parents 'were respected for their gravity and honest life'.[3] He went first to the grammar school in the city and from there to St John's College, Cambridge, where he studied for his BA degree, before going on to Oxford to graduate as MA. He was extremely proud of having attended both universities. On leaving Oxford he set off on a tour of Europe which took him to Italy, Poland, Denmark and Spain, risky though this last sounds, given the running enmity between the two countries. However, on returning to England some time in 1580 he found it impossible to settle down, took lodgings in London and set about seriously devoting himself to wine, women and poetry. 'At my return I ruffled out in my silks in the habit of a malcontent and seemed so discontent that no place would please me to abide in nor no vocation cause me to stay myself in.' A couple of years later, having run through all his money, he returned to Norwich, spent some time in Cambridge, then courted and married 'a gentleman's daughter from Lincolnshire', a pretty fair-haired young woman by the name of Dorothy, and made an attempt at settling down with her in Norwich. Within a year or so she had borne him a daughter and gone home to mother and he was back in London. 'I deserted her', he told his friends, 'because she tried to reform me.' It might be said here that however badly Peele and Greene might have behaved separately, when they came together as they frequently did, they were worse than the sum of their parts.

The youngest of the Wits, born in 1567, was Thomas Nashe, born in Lowestoft in Suffolk. He was the son of a parson, William Nashe, who at that time was in straitened circumstances (presumably Lowestoft was a poor parish), and his second wife, Margaret. When he was six the family moved to the rectory at West Harling, which appears to have brought with it a better stipend. It is possible that he was educated at home by his father, but whether at home or at a local school, when he went up to St John's College, Cambridge, money was still tight, so much so that he was of necessity a 'sizar' student. Sizar students were those too poor to pay fees or who had no scholarship and undertook menial tasks as servants to pay their way, in Nashe's case cleaning and serving in the college itself. A graphic and bitter account of what being such a student entailed is given by the Elizabethan doctor and astrologer, Simon Forman, in his own biography.[4] The only way he and a friend could go up to Oxford was as servants to two wealthy young layabouts. They were forced to fit their studying around running errands, keeping their masters in food and drink, waiting on them hand and foot and assisting them in their assignations with young women. The two young men in question later took Holy Orders, one becoming a bishop, while Forman, with insufficient time to study, had to drop out. Nashe, however, stuck with it. It might be that it was in Cambridge that he first met Greene, who was spending time there between returning from his travels and his marriage. He would almost certainly have known Christopher Marlowe, who was three years ahead of him. In 1588, having taken his degree, Nashe too made his way to London.

So to two of those outside the circle of the Wits. George Chapman was born in Hitchen, Hertfordshire, about 1560. He was the son of Thomas and Joan Chapman and grandson to 'George Nodes, Sergeant to the Buckhounds to Henry VIII'. He too had been up to Oxford and gained his degree but unlike Peele, Greene or Nashe he did not make his way straight to London but entered the service of Sir Robert Sadler and served him as a soldier in the Low Countries. Such close contact with real life and the horrors of war might well account for his more sober outlook on life. Thomas Kyd, born in 1558, had no distance to travel to reach his final destination for he was born in the City and baptised on 6 November, just eleven days before Queen Elizabeth came to the throne. His father, Francis Kyd, was also a scrivener, writer of the Court letter of London and a Freeman of the Company of Scriveners, his mother Joan the legatee of a publisher. At the age of seven he was sent to the Merchant Taylors' School where the headmaster, Dr Richard Mulcaster, was a formidable scholar with a real interest in drama, so the young Thomas learned French, Italian and Spanish as well as the more usual Greek and Latin and must have been introduced to a variety of plays; but although Merchant Taylors had forty-three scholarship places reserved for bright boys at St John's College, Oxford, Kyd never went up to university. As a result of this he was unfairly looked down on by his more snobbish contemporaries, even though the profession of a scrivener and copyist at a time when most of the populace was illiterate was not only essential but highly respected. Both Greene and Nashe made snide comments about Kyd, although it could just be that jealousy also entered into it for Kyd's *The Spanish Tragedy* was the single most popular and successful play of its day, remaining in repertoire for thirty years after his death.

But soon it was clear that there were two dramatists who stood out well above the rest. In 1564, within a few weeks of each other, the young wives of two craftsmen each gave birth to a healthy son. Although one lived in Kent and the other in Warwickshire the two families had much in common. In both cases the father had been apprenticed in leatherwork, one then specialising in shoemaking, the other in glove-making and tanning. Both men, at the time of the birth of their eldest sons, were in comfortable circumstances although each would later run into debt, due in no small part to their predilection for litigation.

Katherine Marlowe's child was born at the very beginning of February but, as is usually the case, there is no exact birth date as it was not until the nineteenth century that births had to be officially registered. The only record of the birth of a child was when it was baptised and its baptism recorded in the Parish Register, known popularly as 'the Church Book'. As baptism was considered essential for eternal life and infant mortality was extremely high, the ceremony usually took place as soon as was practicable, generally about three days after birth. Indeed the Book of Common Prayer bade parents not to postpone christening their child beyond the first Sunday or Holy Day after its birth. Katherine's son, given the name of Christopher after his paternal grandfather, was duly baptised at the Church of St George the Martyr on 6 February. That the baby was safely delivered must have been a considerable relief as her first child, Mary, had died almost immediately after birth.

The Marlowes were established Canterbury craftsmen and Katherine's husband, John, was the third generation to go into the family business, while the grandfather, Christopher, was considered a 'warm man', with a substantial town house in the city and a further property in the Kent countryside consisting of a meadow and twenty acres of grazing rights. John had married Katherine Urry, a Dover girl, on 22 May 1560 at the church where her children would later be baptised. Their home was a fine one in the main street, renowned in its day for carved panelling of such beauty that it attracted a great deal of local envy. It stood on the corner of St George's Street and Little George's Lane but both it and the church, apart from its tower, were destroyed in wartime bombing.

Mary Shakespeare's son was born in April in the family home in Henley Street in the little market town of Stratford-upon-Avon. She had married her husband, also a John, in 1557. John Shakespeare was born in the village of Snitterfield, his father being a tenant farmer on the Asby estate which belonged to the Arden family. John, the first of his family to be apprenticed into leatherwork, had been sent to Stratford to serve his apprenticeship and, once eligible to call himself a master craftsman, he set up in his own right as a glover and tanner and later also as a trader in wool. We know he acquired his first Henley Street house some time in 1552 at an annual ground rent of sixpence, for he is recorded as being fined that year for making a dunghill in the street outside his door instead of under the trees at the end of it like everyone else. John Shakespeare did so well that a few years later he acquired the house next door and knocked the two together to make one substantial property. The second house also had the benefit of a garden at a ground rent of thirteen pence a year.

Mary Shakespeare (née Arden) of Asby was an excellent match for any craftsman, and was very definitely well above John's station in life. She was the daughter of his father's landlord and came from a family who were said to have been great lords in Warwickshire before the Conquest. She was the eighth child and her father's favourite, so much so that, almost unbelievably, when he died he left her not only money but the entire Asby estate and the home farm, now known as 'Mary Arden's House'. This she brought with her into her marriage, along with a hefty dowry. She too must have awaited the birth of her son with no little anxiety for her first baby, a daughter called Joan, had also died shortly after her birth just like little Mary Marlowe. Tradition has it that William Shakespeare was born on 23 April, St George's Day (also the date of his death), and that might well be the case for his baptism is duly recorded in the parish Register of Holy Trinity Church on the 26th.

Both boys proved to be strong and healthy; had they not been, then the history of English literature in general and the theatre in particular would have been very different. When they reached the age of seven both left the dame schools where they had learned the alphabet, numbers and other basics from their horn books and went on to their respective local grammar schools. Both the King's School in Canterbury and the Edward VI Grammar School in Stratford would have offered virtually the same curriculum in which the entire syllabus was based on Latin. In the Lower School they would have come into contact too with the Roman plays of Terence and Plautus. In the Upper School they were introduced to Ovid, alongside more Latin, some Greek, and Rhetoric. Although Holinshed's *Chronicles*, so rich a source for Shakespeare, were published while he was still at school it is unlikely they were part of the syllabus, history generally being taught from the works of Plutarch or the earlier Hall's *Chronicle*.

It was at the age of thirteen that the boys' lives diverged dramatically. Marlowe remained where he was at the King's School in Canterbury until he was fifteen; then, after winning a scholarship designed for those destined to take Holy Orders, he went up to Corpus Christi College, Cambridge. It is difficult to imagine a less appropriate profession than that of the priesthood. Marlowe's subsequent immediate career is relatively well known, in no small part due to the number of books which appeared on the four hundredth centenary of his death in 1993. His questing and adventurous mind soon ensured that he stood out among his contemporaries and quite early on he became the friend, possibly the lover, of Thomas Walsingham. Thomas, who would remain Marlowe's patron until the latter's death, was nephew to Sir Francis Walsingham, the Queen's spymaster. Sir Francis was on the lookout for bright young professionals to act as secret agents, rather than the ragtag of informers and intelligencers who made up most of the secret service of the day, and it is assumed that Thomas introduced his friend to his uncle. It is easy to see why espionage would appeal to Marlowe, who had supreme confidence in his own intellect and ability to outmatch anyone that might be set against him. Thus he was drawn into Walsingham's net and into that shadowy world, both exciting and enticing, from which those who enter can never properly escape.

From then on his story has overtones of a thriller, for twice while he was up at university he disappeared completely without any explanation, on the first occasion for seven weeks during his second year 1582/3, then again for over half a term during his final year when he was taking his MA. He went down from Cambridge for good at the end of the Lent Term of 1584 and duly applied for his MA to be granted to him, but it was withheld by the university authorities on the grounds that he had spent insufficient time at his studies. What happened next is unprecedented.

In a letter to the college authorities from Walsingham on behalf of the Privy Council, he informs them that 'whereas it was reported that Christopher Marlowe was determined to have gone beyond the seas to Rheims and there remain, their Lordships thought it good to certify that he had no such intent; but that in all his actions he had behaved himself orderly and discreetly, whereby he had done her Majesty good service and deserved to be rewarded for his faithful dealing'. Therefore Marlowe should be granted his MA and any rumours that he was frittering away his time on the continent quashed 'by all possible means. . . . Because it was not her Majesty's pleasure that anyone employed, as he had been, in matters touching the benefit of his country should be defamed by those that are ignorant of the affairs he went about.'[5]

In other words, Marlowe had been spying for England. The reference to Rheims suggests that he had been attending the Catholic

Seminary there, founded by the Englishman, Dr Allen, and originally situated in Douai but more recently moved to Rheims. The seminary was a centre for disaffected English students drawn to the old Faith and was notorious as a hotbed of intrigue and a powerhouse for plots. Allen and his colleagues did not only support Philip II in his proposed invasion of England, but actively assisted those plotting to put Mary Stuart on the English throne. What better way was there of discovering what was going on there than by infiltrating an agent into the seminary in the guise of a dissident Catholic student? Another reason for thinking that this is what he was doing was that in *The Jew of Malta* he has his villain, Barabas the Jew, discuss the merits of poisoning the public wells in order to cause the maximum public panic, the possibility of which was under serious discussion in Rheims at the time.

Becoming a secret agent was not the only major difference between Marlowe and the rest of the new theatrical professionals. He was almost certainly gay and, unlike his contemporaries, he had already made waves as a dramatist and poet before he had even come down from Cambridge. His physical and mental energy must have been prodigious for as well as studying, taking his two degrees and spying for Walsingham, he found time to translate Ovid's erotic verse, adapt Virgil's *Tragedy of Dido* for the stage and write the first part of *Tamburlaine*. The play, which introduced theatre-goers to Marlowe's 'mighty line', was first performed in 1587 and became an immediate smash hit rocketing him into celebrity status, a position of which he took every advantage.

Compared to Marlowe, William Shakespeare's journey to the London playhouses was slow and is largely unknown, as is how he was drawn to the theatre in the first place. One incident which occurred in Stratford when he was fifteen years old is worth recording. Shortly before Christmas 1579 the body of a young girl was found in the River Avon, caught under the bare branches of the willows at Tiddington. It was thought she went into the water on 17 December, but the inquest was not held until 11 February 1580 and it is suggested therefore that in the meantime she was temporarily buried. At the end of the hearing the twelve members of the jury, having heard all the evidence, brought in a verdict of accidental death. It was decided that 'she, going with a milk pail to draw water from the river Avon, and standing on the bank of the same, suddenly and by accident, slipped and fell into the river and was drowned *and met her death in no other wise or fashion*' (my italics).[6] The latter phrase suggests that there were those who said otherwise, rumours of suicide after being jilted by a lover perhaps? But the jury had obviously given her the benefit of the doubt. Had they brought in a suicide verdict the result would have been a hasty re-interment at some nearby crossroads after the Coroner had announced that the deceased 'regardless of salvation of her soul and led astray by the instigation of the Devil, threw herself into the water and wilfully drowned herself', thus forfeiting her right to burial in hallowed ground. Why this sad little story is apposite is because the girl's name was Katherine Hamlet and her death and subsequent burial recalls that of Ophelia.

Shakespeare, after leaving school at thirteen, went into the family business. The story of how at the age of eighteen he got the much older Anne Hathaway pregnant, subsequently married her in a ceremony which had all the hallmarks of a shotgun wedding presided over by her brothers, of the birth of that child, Elizabeth, followed by twins, Hamnet and Judith, and his subsequent disappearance from Stratford is too well known to go into further. All we know for sure is that he went away leaving his parents to care for his deserted wife and children, no small responsibility for Mary Shakespeare who still had small children of her own. Shakespeare's supposedly 'missing years' have given rise to a wide variety of theories based on his subsequent work: that he was a soldier in the Low Countries (*Henry V*), studied at the Inns of Court (*The Merchant of Venice*), went to sea (*Pericles* and *The Tempest*), was employed as a tutor by Lord Strange in Derbyshire (any play involving comic schoolmasters) and, of course, that hoary old chestnut, that he simply ran off to London after having been caught poaching on the Lucy estate at Charlecote, just outside Stratford, and then stood around outside the Globe holding the horses of those attending performances until someone noticed him, a theory which falls down somewhat when we know he was in London ten years before the Globe was even built.

There is a more prosaic and practical possibility. Since nobody knows when Shakespeare actually left Stratford it could well be that the 'missing years' were few. During 1587 five different theatre companies visited Stratford, one of which was the Queen's Men in June. They arrived in the town two men short for, while they were performing in Oxford, one of their actors, William Knell, was killed in a fight with a fellow player, John Towne. In the evidence given at the inquest, held on 13 June in the town of Thame, it was stated that Knell, fighting drunk, had picked a quarrel with Towne and drawn his sword on him. Towne had been forced to defend himself while calling out to Knell to stop the fight. Knell had refused to do so and Towne 'fearing for his life' had struck out and run him through. Towne was therefore now in custody.[7]

Losing two actors would have been pretty disastrous for a small touring company. For Shakespeare, already drawn to the theatre and frustrated with his life in the family business and with his domestic circumstances, such a situation might well have afforded him the opportunity of a lifetime, the chance to learn his new trade on the road for he, like George Peele, was an actor as well as a playwright. There was also another link with the Knell-Towne fight. Shortly before his death, Knell had married a Rebecca Edwards who, a year later, after a decent interval, then married the actor John Hemings, one of Shakespeare's closest friends as well as a colleague. Whatever the real truth of the matter, whether on his own on foot or on horseback, or as part of the company of the Queen's Men, Shakespeare was almost certainly in town to see one of the early performances of *Tamburlaine*.

While their original backgrounds might have been very alike, the characters and personalities of the two young men could hardly have been more dissimilar. Throughout his short life Marlowe was flamboyant, outrageous in his behaviour and opinions, given to outbursts of violence, and courting danger; it was as if from the first he was programmed to self-destruct. Shakespeare, on the other hand, was cautious and hard-working, carefully investing the money he made in property both in London and Stratford, given to romantic attachments and, politically, keeping his head down. But both gave us some of the most wonderful verse ever written.

So, by one means or another, all our first wave of dramatists and their associates, the poets, essayists and pamphleteers, were ensconced in London by Armada year, objects of both envy and antipathy. There are plenty of examples today of how sudden recognition and fame affects those previously unused to either. To be shot from the obscurity of a distant town or village or the backstreets of London and find your name on every poster or billboard as the writer of the play about which everyone is talking is heady stuff – not to mention that with such fame or notoriety come all the trappings, from fans plying you with drink every time you set foot in a tavern and would-be poets hanging on your every word, to women from all walks of life throwing themselves at you. The nearest analogy today is that of the star footballer or pop idol. It is hardly surprising therefore that there were those who would be destroyed by it.

THREE

A Theatre for the People

All the world's a stage
And all the men and women merely players . . .
As You Like It, II, vii

The new breed of playwrights was to produce a new breed of actor. We know very little of the actors who played in the early companies unless, like Knell and Towne, they brought attention on themselves for reasons other than by their performances, but with the emergence of more professional companies based in the playhouses and using the services of professional writers, there emerged the actors whose names have come down to us through the centuries, the two greatest of which in their day were Edward Alleyn and Richard Burbage.

Alleyn was born on 1 September 1566 to a Bishopsgate publican who died when Alleyn was four. Shortly afterwards his mother remarried, his new stepfather being a haberdasher. Obviously neither trade appealed to him and what attracted him to the acting profession is not known, but by the time he was sixteen young Edward was touring in Leicestershire with the Earl of Worcester's Company, possibly having joined them first as an apprentice. We know he was in Leicester at this time because he was hauled up with the rest of the players before the local Justices as the company claimed to have lost or mislaid its vital Licence to Perform, which also set out the details of its patron. They had been brought to court because, in spite of this and in defiance of the Lord Mayor of Leicester who presumably had demanded to see it, they went ahead and performed their plays anyway. Afterwards, when they had been suitably admonished, they apologised to his worship and begged him not to tell their patron.[1]

Richard Burbage was born about a year later into the first truly theatrical family, since his father James had built The Theatre and although James is first described as a carpenter he was by that time an established actor and company manager. So young Richard went straight into the business as a boy player and by the age of thirteen even his brothers were describing him as 'brilliant'. While in most cases such praise from within the home might be taken with a pinch of salt, in this instance the description was absolutely justified. It is almost impossible now to imagine what the performances of the sixteenth-century actors were like, except that we know their style was almost certainly declamatory since an actor then needed to hold an audience of hundreds, even thousands, in an open-air environment amid plenty of noise, and that they used an accepted series of gestures to denote fear, love, anger and other emotions. It would have been impossible, for example, for Burbage, when playing Hamlet, to lurk behind a pillar and in quiet anguish ask himself 'to be or not to be, that is the question'. He would have had to stride out to the front of the stage and project his soliloquy right up to the top gallery. And although in terms of some of the great twentieth-century actors, Alleyn has been likened in style to Sir John Gielgud and Burbage, who played a far wider variety of roles, to Sir Laurence Olivier, one of Alleyn's most famous parts was Marlowe's Tamburlaine, a mighty despot who set out to conquer the known world, and he was obviously capable of convincing his audience that he was capable of it.

Backing up the two stars was a substantial second rank of good actors such as Henry Condell and John Hemings, who later put together and published Shakespeare's plays. However it was the comic actors who, like Alleyn and Burbage, were to become household names: the 'clowns' Richard Tarlton, Will Kempe and Robert Armin. These clowns were not the white-faced creatures of the circus but much more like the comedians of the nineteenth-century music halls or today's stand-up comics, and they were hugely popular. Tarlton had been a publican, first in Colchester, then in London where he kept the Saba Inn. He also ran an ordinary in Paternoster Row. He first took up acting in 1577 and by 1583 was one of the twelve founder members of the Queen's Men. He had a number of famous acts, including one as a drunk and another, in which he made use of his dog, was said greatly to amuse the Queen and it has been suggested that Shakespeare wrote the part of Launce (who is accompanied by a dog) in *Two Gentlemen of Verona*, especially for Tarlton. His fame became such that, even in an era when communication was poor, it spread nationwide, so much so that folk living far from London and unlikely ever to journey more than a few miles from their town or village, would tell each other his best-known jokes. It was said of him that he only had to walk on to a stage for an audience to collapse with laughter, one playgoer, Henry Peacham, writing:

> Tarleton, when his head was only seen,
> The Tirehouse door and tapestry between,
> Set all the multitude in such a laughter,
> They could not hold for scarce an hour after.

He was particularly famous for the 'jigs' which he performed at the end of the show, song and dance acts which were often cheeky, satirical and risqué. He also played parts in various dramas, even writing one of his own, *The Seven Deadly Sins*, but it is likely that, ad libber that he was, he found sticking to a set script difficult and was likely to have been a loose cannon among the more serious actors who had carefully learned set lines and where to stand on the stage to say them.

Of William Kempe and Robert Armin we know considerably less. Kempe's main claim to fame is that he left the theatre to dance a widely reported 'jig' from London to Norwich, that he wrote an entertainment called *Nine Days Wonder* and played the comic roles in Shakespeare's early works, such as Peter in *Romeo and Juliet* and Dogberry in *Much Ado About Nothing*. He is also credited, perhaps wrongly, with being the original of the actor criticised by Hamlet for speaking far more than has been set down for him. Robert Armin, on the other hand, was not so much a clown as an actor capable of more than comedy since legend has it that he played both the Fool in *King Lear* and Feste in *Twelfth Night*, and to do so convincingly he must have had a more serious side to his talent. He also wrote plays of his own, one of which has the self-explanatory title *The Two Maids of More-Clacke*.

The common factor binding so many theatre people together in the early days, the dramatists, actors, costume and prop makers, and inventors of special effects, was, undoubtedly, that great entrepreneur Philip Henslowe. Anyone who saw the film *Shakespeare in Love* must have laughed heartily at the opening sequence in which Henslowe is seen with his booted feet being held over a fire by his creditors who are demanding money from him. In real life, however, he was a great deal more canny. It is little short of a miracle that so many of his papers dealing with the day-to-day running of the Rose Theatre and his association with writers and actors, along with notes and letters, survive to this day and are the single best contemporary source of how the Elizabethan theatre actually operated. The diaries and papers first came to light in the eighteenth century and were found lying among others of lesser interest in the library of Dulwich College. The various 'books' of the *Diary* had started out as a record of Henslowe's brother's interests in mining and smelting in the Ashdown Forest between the years 1576 to 1581, but they were then passed on to Philip, who used them initially to record the income and expenditure of his timber business and only later for details of his theatrical activities.

From 1582 onwards, therefore, he records which plays were in repertoire, how much was taken at the door, notes of advances made to dramatists commissioned to write plays on the basis of a synopsis or 'plot which they had presented to him' (a truly revolutionary notion), inventories of costumes, scenery and props, along with what he had paid out for the equipment necessary for special effects. There are also a fair number of critical comments, not least when he had to bail a writer or actor out of gaol, most often for being either drunk or disorderly or after they had been arrested for debt.

He also fancied himself as something of a physician and there are a number of notes of the remedies that took his fancy which he might well have inflicted on his actors, such as 'take ants and stamp on them, then strain them through a cloth and mix with swine's grease, then stamp on knot grass the same and take the juice and mix with strainings of eggs and put in the ear which will help cure deafness'. Another 'cure' consisted of frying earthworms 'a dozen times at least' and pounding up the mess to make an ointment, or mixing a variety of herbs and flowers before boiling them all up 'with the urine of a boy'. Therefore it comes as no little surprise to discover that when it came to his own health Henslowe was not averse to consulting his local doctor, Simon Forman, for more professional advice, and his various complaints, and Forman's remedies for them, are duly recorded in the latter's *Casebooks*. He was also deeply superstitious and there is a section on useful spells to ward off everything from the evil eye and the plague to 'making a fowl fall dead'. Would that such a record had come down to us from the Burbages.[2]

Even without having his boots set on fire, the real Henslowe appears in the *Diaries* as a somewhat comic figure with an eye to the main chance, as is shown by his absolute determination to become the Queen's own bear-keeper, an ambition which seems to have been far more important to him than any desire to go down in history as the person who first brought together so much talent and put it on the stage. For it is a simple fact that just about every playwright of any note wrote first for Henslowe, many having their plays performed by the Lord Admiral's Men, the company with which he was most closely associated. Among these was the young William Shakespeare with the *Henry VI* trilogy, in the writing of which it is thought he was assisted by others including Marlowe; also *Titus Andronicus* which is entirely his own work. Both were written before he moved on rapidly to become Burbage's house playwright, a position he was to hold for over twenty years, making him a unique figure in the dramatic world of his day.

Of the two sober dramatists outside the circle of Wits, Chapman and Kyd, Chapman did not begin to write seriously for the theatre until the mid-1590s, partly because he needed to earn money elsewhere since, careful and industrious as he was, he had somehow ended up in the clutches of a notorious money-lender, John Wolfall, and was to spend the next twenty years desperately trying to pay off the debt. It was left, ironically, to the hard-working, self-effacing, mocked 'little scrivener', Thomas Kyd, to invent a whole, new and exciting genre. His *Spanish Tragedy*, first performed in 1591 and one of Henslowe's biggest hits, ushered in the popular genre now known as the Revenge Plays, establishing a formula which most follow, beginning with either the ghost of a victim, or a relation or lover associated with him, explaining to the audience the events, which have resulted in his becoming a 'revenger'. The scene is set therefore, as in a Greek tragedy, for a predictable set of events at the end of which the villain or villains pay the price for their crime. En route to the denouement the audience is treated to more murders and sudden deaths, often devised in highly ingenious ways.

The Spanish Tragedy opens with the ghost of Andrea, recently killed in Spain's war with Portugal, complaining to the Spirit of Revenge that it has so far done nothing to bring to book those who have murdered his son. After further discussion, the chosen revenger is Hieronimo (or Jeronimo), Marshal of Spain, thus setting him on a course of bloodshed and mayhem which ends with the popular device of a play within a play revealing all. Hieronimo bites off his tongue in order to keep silent as to his motive, although he kindly explains to the audience before doing so. Grand Guignol it might be, but it was wildly popular with audiences and the character of Hieronimo made sufficient impact for the character to be referred to in subsequent plays well after Kyd's death. He is also generally given the credit for writing an early version of *Hamlet*, known as the *Urr-Hamlet*. Nashe, writing of Kyd in his usual disparaging manner, notes: 'Yet the English Seneca, read by candlelight, yields many good sentences, as "blood is a beggar", and so forth: and if you entreat him fair in a frosty morning, he will afford you whole Hamlets, I should say handfuls of tragical speeches . . .'.[3] Other commentators describe the play opening with a ghost, robed in a white sheet and clanking with chains, calling out 'revenge, revenge!' However, since the text is long since lost there is no way of knowing how much Shakespeare took from it.

The point should be made that virtually none of the early professional playwrights would have arrived at the Rose or The

Theatre clutching the synopsis, or 'plot', of a truly original play in their hands. The vast majority of the drama of the day was taken from a wide variety of sources, many of them well known at least to those who were literate. From their grammar schools they would have been familiar with the comic works of Plautus, the tragedies of Seneca, with Ovid and Greek drama, all read in the original. They could also draw on the historian Raphael Holinshed's *Chronicles*, the source for so many history plays, which was first published in 1575 and added to in 1586, not to mention Chaucer, Boccaccio and Italian literature, and the popular stories, fairy tales and legends of heroes and romantic love told around many a winter hearth.

Lyly offered his audiences dramatic presentations of the latter, the earliest of which was *The Woman in the Moon*, and the most popular *Mother Bombie*. Peele's first known play, *The Arraignment of Paris*, based on the Greek myth, was first performed in 1581, three years after The Theatre had been built. It is highly likely that he also took a role in it since for the previous two years he had needed to support himself following a court case on 19 September 1579 when his father was bound over to discharge from his house before Michaelmas 'his son, George Peele, and all other of his household which have been chargeable to him'; in other words Peele's rowdy lifestyle, and the kind of friends he brought home with him, did not go down at all well with Christ's Hospital's governing body. He went on to join the company of the Lord Admiral's Men, remaining with them as a player until 1589 when his circumstances improved after he married a lady who brought him a dowry of both land and property. Yet in spite of his dissolute reputation the only play of his that has come down to us more or less intact is his charming and amusing *Old Wives' Tale*, in which two young men lost in a forest are taken in by an old woman who regales them with a series of popular tales which are duly acted out for the audience, including allusions to Celtic mythology where disembodied heads in wells converse and offer advice to various characters. We know from Henslowe's *Diaries* that it was very popular, along with his patriotic piece, *The Battle of Alcazar*, and a biblical play on the subject of David and Bathsheba, which have not survived.

Greene too wrote lively and popular lightweight pieces based around popular tales, the best known being the comedies *Friar Bacon and Friar Bungay* and *George a Green, the Pindar of Wakefield*. He took the Italian play *Orlando Furioso*, made it his own and sold the exclusive rights twice. He also supplemented his income, as did many others including Nashe and Thomas Dekker, writing pamphlets, the most popular of which, *A Notable Discovery of Cosenage*, dedicated to 'Gentlemen Readers', purports to warn readers of the dangers and immorality of the Elizabethan underworld, which he describes in vivid detail, thus ensuring its popularity under the pretence that he is merely exposing sin.

As well as borrowing ideas from past writers, there were also rewrites of plays already in the early repertoires such as *The Famous Victories of Henry V* (in which Tarlton took a role), *The True Tragedy of Richard III*, *King Leir and his Three Daughters* and *The Troublesome Reign of King John*, the last attributed to John Bale who died in 1563, who wrote a number of plays to be performed by children. All three were, of course, seized on later by Shakespeare. Elizabethan audiences enjoyed a good murder story just as much as the Victorian playgoers who flocked to melodramas like *Murder in the Red Barn* and *Sweeney Todd* or today's addicts of 'true crime' series.

One such is the anonymous play *Arden of Faversham*, dating from about 1587, which was regularly in the repertoire of the Lord Admiral's Men and much of which falls into the realm of black comedy, even if the reality was not so amusing. On St Valentine's Day 1551 Thomas Arden of Faversham in Kent, Chief Controller of HM Customs, was found dead outside his house after his wife, Alice, had made several attempts to do away with him. She was considerably younger than him and was already involved in an affair with the family steward, Mosbie, before the marriage took place. The drama details her various attempts to get rid of Arden, starting with poisoning his gruel, and ending with her employing a couple of hit men to do the deed for a fee of £10. If the play is to be believed they were incredibly inept and every one of their increasingly desperate attempts failed. Finally Mosbie and Alice concealed them in the house and arranged for Arden to be home playing a game of chess, during which 'Black Will' would creep up behind him and do the deed. But Will bungles it again, leaving Mosbie to 'stroke Arden on the head' – with a 14lb weight! They then lug the body outside, not taking into account that it is snowing and that their bloodstained footprints will lead the authorities directly to the corpse. The play ends there but in reality the aftermath was grim; Alice was burned at the stake, the punishment for murderous wives, her maid suffering a similar fate. A chilling item in the Canterbury town record notes: 'for the charges of burning Mistress Arden and the Execution of Geo. Bradshaw – thirteen shillings'. Mosbie was hanged and as for Black Will, he disappeared and was never seen again. A slightly later play, also anonymous and based on a real incident, is *A Yorkshire Tragedy*, in which a feckless, violent and jealous husband kills two of his children, attempts to murder his wife and baby, then turns his knife on himself.

It was Marlowe, though, who stood head and shoulders above his immediate contemporaries with his poetic 'mighty line'. He brought about a sea change in writing for the theatre. Compared to Shakespeare and the second wave of dramatists that were to come, his plays have no complex plots or subplots but consist almost entirely of a sequence of events in which we follow the course set by the protagonist, Tamburlaine, Edward II, Barabas the Jew and Faustus. What is without question is that his plays had an enormous influence on what came after. It was the first part of *Tamburlaine*, written while he was still at Cambridge and put on by Henslowe, which first gave Marlowe his soaring reputation as a popular dramatist whose work audiences flocked to see.

The original for Tamburlaine was Timur, the fourteenth-century son of a Mongol chief who fought his way west, laying waste everything as he went. When the citizens of Baghdad stood in his way, he razed the city to the ground and massacred all the inhabitants. Timur was reputedly both ugly and lame, but Marlowe's character is whole and handsome, sweeping him across the known world bringing war, murder, torture and slavery until he finally meets the only enemy he is unable to conquer: death. He is the first of Marlowe's great overreachers. 'Is it not passing brave to be a king, And ride in triumph through Persopolis?' he asks, to which the king in whom he is confiding replies: 'To be a king is half to be a god'. 'A god', responds Tamburlaine, 'is not so glorious as a king'.

Tamburlaine also produced what must be one of the first great catchphrases in popular use. There are a number of scenes in which Tamburlaine is brought on in triumph, the most famous being that in which he is dragged across the stage in a chariot hauled by four kings, bridled like horses, whipping them on and shouting 'Holla, ye pampered jades of Asia!' For some reason the phrase really tickled the fancy of audiences who found the notion of royalty being used as horses and described as 'pampered jades' highly amusing, given the casual violence of the day. So popular was it that it also crops up years later in different contexts in plays by Marlowe's contemporaries. Tamburlaine was one of Edward Alleyn's greatest roles and we know he played the part wearing a magnificent suit of clothes, with red velvet breeches, for it is listed in Henslowe's inventories of costumes; also that there was a splendid saddle for Tamburlaine's use. Nor was any effort spared with the special effects for during one of the earliest performances real bullets were used, with the result that during the scene in which the Governor of Babylon is executed, one went astray and killed a member of the audience.

But while popular audiences continued to increase, there were still those who criticised either the content or, more often, theatre in general. Sir Philip Sidney, who considered himself a cut above the fare being presented to the populace (although he had actually stood godfather to Tarlton's son), was a stern critic of popular drama. The new playwrights, he complained, no longer always observe 'the rules of honest civility nor skilful poetry' as set down by Aristotle, where all the action must take place within 'the compass of a single day and in one place':

Now [he grumbles] one side of the stage may be Asia, the other Africa, along with so many underkingdoms that the Player, when he comes in, must ever begin with telling where he is, or else the

Part of a sixteenth-century map of London, showing the theatres on the South Bank.

tale will not be conceived [understood]. Then there shall be, say, three ladies who walk to gather flowers, and then we believe the stage to be a garden. By and by we hear news of a shipwreck in the same place, and then we are to blame if we accept it not for a rock upon the back of which comes out a hideous monster with fire and smoke . . . meanwhile two armies fly in, represented with but four swords and bucklers, and then what hard heart will not receive it for a pitched battle? Next comes the love interest in which a gallant young prince marries, is then lost leaving his wife to bear him a son who, in turn, grows up and falls in love and so on and so on and all this in two hours space.[4]

The real loathing shown by those who hated the whole idea of professional theatre is well summed up in a pamphlet published by the Bristol cleric, John Northbrooke, in 1577, which was still being reprinted and circulated in London as late as 1592. For Northbrooke the stage was 'a spectacle and a school for all wickedness' for those who went to the playhouse:

if you will learn how to be false, and deceive your husbands, or husbands their wives, how to play the harlot to obtain anyone's love, how to ravish, how to beguile, how to betray, flatter, lie, swear, foreswear, how to allure to whoredom, how to murder, how to poison, how to disobey and to rebel against Princes, to consume treasures prodigally, to move to lusts, to ransack and spoil cities and towns, to be idle and blaspheme, to sing filthy songs of love and speak filthy.[5]

Few, however, were listening.

Many of the dramatists and actors were still living north of the Thames in the late 1580s and early 1590s, although gradually they would move over the river with the building of the Hope and Globe theatres and the demise of The Theatre. A mid-sixteenth-century map of the city of London and its environs, with the streets in which they lived, shows a wide variety of green spaces open to those living north of the river, of which the most prominent is Finsbury Fields with its windmills, beside which are little figures carrying bags of grain. It was also a popular place for women to hang out the laundry not, as today, on washing lines but over bushes. 'The white sheet bleaching on the hedge', the rogue and petty thief Autolycus sings in *The Winter's Tale* as he stuffs one into his bag, prompting Simon Forman, on returning from a performance of the play, to note that he must 'beware all such thieving fellows'. It was a good place too for the exchange of gossip for there is a drawing of women sitting on the grass chatting while behind them two young men struggle along under the weight of a full basket of garments which is slung on poles between their shoulders, the sort of laundry basket later used by Shakespeare in the *Merry Wives of Windsor*. To the east are the Spital Fields where young men went to practise sword fighting and archery or even fought duels.

Few of the dramatists were making large sums of money from their trade but their flamboyance, increasing reputation and high profiles, with their names posted on playbills, ensured that they were noticed. Both playwrights and actors acquired followings, not least among the wives of respectable artisans and merchants, some of whom were prepared to pursue the objects of their admiration. Both Greene and Peele, in spite of their appalling lifestyles, were sufficiently attractive to women to marry money, even if Greene's marriage proved short-lived after he moved in with Emma Ball, the sister of 'Cutting Ball Jack', the notorious highwayman. His nickname derives from what he threatened to do to those gentlemen who would not pay up. As for Shakespeare, his earliest lodgings were just off Bishopsgate which we know because at some stage he went off to live elsewhere without paying the equivalent of his rates and was pursued by the authorities for its recovery. It was during this time, depending on which academic's view you accept, that he was taken up with his passionate affair with the Dark Lady of the Sonnets.

Marlowe, whose proclivities were somewhat different, was either sharing lodgings with his friend, the poet Thomas Watson, in Norton Folgate, or was his close neighbour, although he was exceptionally fortunate not only to be able to bask in success but also because Thomas Walsingham's fine mansion out at Scadbury was always available to him, along with financial assistance should he need it. It also gave him something really precious: privacy and quietness in which to write. The others had to make do as best they could, the worst off having to share bedrooms and even beds. It is hard to imagine what it must have been like to try and write a five-act drama by hand, using only ink and a quill pen, on any flat surface available and most likely surrounded by constant noise and interruption, not to mention having to rewrite and change whole scenes backstage at the theatre during rehearsal when Burbage or Alleyn felt something had not worked properly or whole pages to fit in with a particular production.

But for all of them the theatrical world had provided more than any could have imagined as schoolboys. From being just another anonymous boy growing up in the City or the son of an artisan craftsman in a small town or rural village, known only to immediate friends and neighbours, they were caught up in the excitement of creative activity, working with actors on a drama and finally seeing their work in production, able to stand inside and watch the reaction of a live audience to their latest play. It must have been heady stuff. Not to mention strolling into the nearest tavern or ordinary afterwards to accept the praise or criticism of those who had spent the afternoon in the playhouse, while looking across at the young women whose eyes were full of promise. Actors and writers had finally come together at the right time and in the right place, not only in the playhouses, but also in the society in which they moved, providing them with the opportunity to spark ideas off each other as they met up in the ordinaries, inns and taverns of Shoreditch and the Bankside.

FOUR

Men About Town

See you him yonder who sits o'er the stage.
With the Tobacco pipe now at his mouth?

Everard Guilpin, *Skialetheia* (1598)

It is left to two popular playwrights to tell us something of what it was like to live in their London, the London of the theatre, the underworld (with the denizens of which they freely mixed), and how to get around and cut a dash even if hard up: Robert Greene and Thomas Dekker – Greene for his streetwise advice to an innocent abroad on the perils awaiting him, Dekker for his wonderfully funny description of a day in the life of an indigent writer about town. Both Greene's supposedly cautionary pamphlet and Dekker's hilarious advice to his protégé offer a picture of the capital during the last decade of the sixteenth century that no amount of academic research or learned surmise can possibly surpass. Greene's *A Notable Discovery of Cosenage, Conie-catchers and Crossbiters*[1] was published in 1592, shortly before his death, and Dekker's *A Gull's Horn Book*[2] was first published about ten years later but little, if anything, had changed in the intervening period.

Greene needs no further introduction. Thomas Dekker, about whose origins we know very little until he started writing professionally, was born in London sometime in 1570. As well as delightful comedies such as *The Shoemaker's Holiday* and collaborations with other dramatists on a wide variety of work, like a number of his contemporaries he wrote popular pamphlets which would sell for a few pence. His is a name which fairly regularly appears in *Henslowe's Diary* when he runs into money problems.

48

To begin with Greene and the Elizabethan underworld, those to whom his pamphlet is addressed need look no further for practical advice on the perils awaiting the unwary on the streets, inns and taverns of even the better parts of London, let alone the brothels and gaming houses of the Bankside:

The cony-catchers, apparelled like honest civil gentlemen or good fellows, with smooth face, as if butter would not melt in their mouths, after dinner when the clients are come from Westminster Hall and are at leisure to walk up and down Paul's, Fleet Street, Holborn, the Strand, and such common-haunted places, where these cozening companions attend only to spy out a prey; who, as soon as they see a plain country fellow, well and clean apparelled, either in a coat of homespun russet or of frieze, as the time requires, and a side-pouch at his side – 'There is a cony', saith one. [The most obvious hazard is the pickpocket or cutpurse]

In St. Paul's between ten and eleven is their hour and there they walk, and perhaps if there be a great press, strike a stroke in the middle walk, that is upon some plain man that stands gazing about, having never seen the church before; but their chiefest time is at divine service, when men devoutly go up to hear either a sermon, or else the harmony of the choir and organs. There the nip and foist [cutpurse and pickpocket], as devoutly as if he were some zealous person, standeth soberly with his eyes elevated to heaven, when his hand is either on the purse or in the pocket, surveying every corner of it for coin.

Then, of course, there are the whores, known on the Bankside as the 'Winchester Geese' since they operated on the substantial area of church-owned land within the borough of Southwark which was under the jurisdiction of the Bishop of Winchester. Greene was an expert on whores, which is not surprising as for several years he lived and was kept by one. 'A shameless hussy has honey in her lips', he warns, 'and her mouth is as sweet as honey, her throat as soft as oil; but the end of her is more bitter than aloes and her tongue is more sharp than a two-edged sword.' 'End' has a double meaning in

49

this context. It might well be understood to mean that such a woman would come to a bad end, but it could also be taken as a warning that while her mouth might be sweet as honey, her 'end' was more likely to give you at best 'the clap' (gonorrhoea) or at worse 'the pox' (syphilis). Very aware that sex always sells popular journalism, he pontificates against lust while going into its variations in detail. There is no end to the tricks played by whores, he counsels, from the straightforward stealing of a purse as a client sleeps, to a variation in which the client is set on and robbed by the whore's pimp while she is busy servicing him.

He particularly warns against 'cross-biting', a ploy still used centuries later and more recently known as 'the badger game'. 'Some unruly mates', he writes, 'that place their content in lust, let slip the liberty of their eyes on some painted beauty, let their eyes stray to their unchaste bosoms til their hearts be set on fire.' They then set about courting the fair one and are almost immediately successful, 'their love need not wait', and the young woman either leads the way to the tavern 'to seal up the match with a bottle of Hippocras, or straight way she takes him to some bad place'. But once the couple have got into bed and are 'set to it', there enters 'a terrible fellow, with side hair and a fearful beard, as though he were one of Polyphemus cut, and he comes frowning in and says "What hast thou to do, base knave, to carry my sister, or my wife?" Or some such . . .' The accomplice then turns on the woman saying she is no better than a whore, and threatens to call a constable immediately and haul them both before the nearest Justice. 'The whore that has tears at command, immediately falls a-weeping and cries him mercy.' The luckless lover, caught in the act, and terrified that his being brought publicly before the Justices will get back to his wife and family, or his lord or his employer, has no option then but to pay up whatever it takes to persuade the 'husband' or 'brother' to keep quiet. At least in Elizabethan London there was no photographer party to the set-up and at hand to take blackmail pictures.

Greene also gives advice against card-sharpers and how they operate, how cards are marked, games fixed, though swiftly adding 'yet, gentlemen, when you shall read this book, written faithfully to discover these cozening practices, think I go not about to disprove or disallow the most ancient and honest pastime or recreation of Card Play . . .', which he could hardly avoid adding for he was a compulsive gambler, another reason why he was always in debt. Overall what his pamphlet shows is how little has changed. It is no surprise to learn, for instance, that the Three Card Trick, or Find the Lady, was as popular a way to part a fool and his money as it is now. He finishes on a warning note, pointing out that his stories of whores, gamesters, picklocks, highway robbers and forgers have been told merely to show how such behaviour leads only to the gallows. Heaven forfend that it might be thought he was writing his pamphlets only to make money.

Dekker assumes the role of both narrator and instructor to his young visitor, one inference being that the young man in question is a would-be writer who has just arrived in town. As narrator he addresses both him and us as 'you' as we follow them through the day from getting up in the morning to falling into bed at night. We take it that his protégé has arranged to meet Dekker at his lodgings, arriving bright and early and eager for instruction. He is therefore somewhat surprised to find his guide and mentor still in bed. Quick as a flash, Dekker extols the virtues of sleeping in:

Do but consider what an excellent thing is sleep. It is an estimable jewel, a tyrant would give his crown for an hour's slumber. It cannot be bought. Of so beautiful a shape is it that even when a man lies with an Empress, he cannot be quiet until he leaves her embracements to rest with sleep. So indebted are we to this kinsman of death, that we owe the better tribute of half our lives to him. He is the golden chain that ties health and our bodies together. [However insomniacs must avoid doctors and their noxious potions for even] Derrick the Hangman of Tyburn cannot turn a man off his perch as fast as one of these breeders of purgation.

After chatting on for some time, he finally gets out of bed and, as he reaches for his clothes and gets dressed, gives his advice on what to wear in order to make an impression.

51

THE GVLS

Horne-booke:

6

Stultorum plena ſunt omnia.

Al Sauio meza parola, Baſta.

By T. Deckar.

Imprinted at London for R. S. 1 6o9.

For it is well to try and dress in the fashion. For instance, one's boots should always be as wide as a wallet and so fringed as to hang down to the ankles. One's doublet of the showiest stuff you can afford. Never cut your hair or suffer a comb to fasten his teeth there. Let it grow thick and bushy, like a forest or some wilderness. Let not those four-footed creatures that breed in it and are tenants to that crown land, be put to death . . . Long hair will make you dreadful to your enemies, manly to your friends; it blunts the edge of the sword and deadens the thump of the bullet; in winter a warm nightcap, in summer a fan of feathers.

Belatedly they leave Dekker's lodgings bound for the first tourist attraction and it is clear the young man is amazed at what he sees, the side aisles of the great church being full of stalls, while the middle one is used by those parading up and down to see and be seen, prompting Dekker to remark: 'Is it not more like a market place than a great house of God?' He leads his protégé to the stalls of those selling fine cloth, loudly insisting that they are looking for velvet or taffeta for a new doublet. If he is worried about wasting their time, then a good ploy is to ask if there is not something even finer to be had than that they have been shown and, after the stallholder has obliged, ordering several yards of the chosen stuff to be paid for and collected later. Failure to collect it is no problem because the stallholder will soon sell it on. He next turns his attention to those walking in the centre aisle, 'the Mediterranean', calling out to all and sundry in a familiar fashion. On someone of note, he advises, 'you should address him familiarly even though he has never seen you before in his life, shouting out loud that he will know where to find you at two o'clock'.

No visit to St Paul's is complete without a trip up the Great Tower which costs tuppence:

As you go up you must count all the stairs to the top and, when you reach it, carve your name on the leads, for how else will it be known that you have been here? For there are more names carved there than in Stowe's Chronicle. [He should take care, though, because the] rails are as rotten as your great-grandfather [and only recently one, Kit Woodroffe, tried to vault over them] and so fell to his death.

By now, of course, it is time for lunch and the two make for an ordinary without further delay. But even entering such a place should be undertaken in a manner designed to draw attention:

Always give the notion you have arrived by horse. Then push through the press, maintaining a swift but ambling pace, your doublet neat, your rapier and poniard in place and, if you have a friend to whom you might fling your cloak for him to carry, all the better. Let him, if possible, be shabbier than yourself and so be a foil to publish you and your clothes the better. Discourse as loud as you can – no matter to what purpose – if you but make a noise and laugh in fashion, and promise for a while, and avoid quarrelling and maiming any, you shall be much observed.

Remind your friend loudly, for instance, of how often you have been under fire from the enemy, of the

hazardous voyages you took with the great Portuguese Navigator, besides your eight or nine small engagements in Ireland and the Low Countries. Talk often of 'his Grace' and how well he regards you and how frequently you dine with the Count of this and that . . . and by all means offer assistance to all and sundry, ask them if they require your good offices at Court? [Or] are there those bowed down and troubled with holding two offices? A vicar with two church livings? You would be only too happy to purchase one.

At this point Dekker suggests his protégé pull a handkerchief out of his pocket, bringing with it a paper which falls to the floor. When it is picked up and handed back to him the response should be:

'Please, I beg you, do not read it!' Try, without success to snatch it back. If all press you as to if it is indeed yours, say, 'faith it is the work of a most learned gentleman and great poet'. This seeming to lay it on another man will be counted either modesty in you, or a sign that you are not ambitious and dare not claim it for fear of its brilliance. If they still wish to hear something, take care you learn by heart some verses of another man's great work and so repeat them. Though this be against all honesty and conscience, it may very well get you the price of a good dinner.

After lunch then where else but to the playhouse? Not to mention advice on how to ruin the performance of an actor, or the reputation of a dramatist, from one who must have suffered the latter at first hand. It must all be planned beforehand. First, the would-be wrecker must not stand with

the common groundlings and gallery commoners, who buy their sport by the penny. . . . Whether you visit a private or public theatre, arrive late. Do not enter until the trumpet has sounded twice. Announce to all that you will sit on the stage, and then haggle loftily over the cost of your stool. Let no man offer to hinder you from obtaining the title of insolent, overweening, coxcomb. Then push with noise, through the crowds to the stage.

So having reached the stage, you clamber on to it, stand in the middle and:

ask loudly whose play it is. If you know not the author rail against him and so behave yourself as to enforce the author to know you. By sitting on the stage, if a knight you may haply get a mistress; if a mere Fleet Street gentleman, a wife; but assure yourself by your continual residence, the first and principal man in election to begin 'we three'. By spreading your body on the stage and being a Justice in the examining of plays, you shall put yourself in such authority that the Poet [dramatist] shall not dare present his piece without your approval.

Before the play actually begins it is a good idea to set up a card game with the others who are seated on the stage:

As you play, shout insults at the gaping ragamuffins and then throw the cards down in the middle of the stage, just as the last sound of trumpet rings out, as though you had lost. [Then, as the] quaking Prologue rubs his cheeks for colour and gives the trumpets their cue for him to enter, point out to your acquaintances a lady in a black-and-yellow striped hat, or some such, shouting to us all that you had ordered the very same design for your mistress and that you had it from your tailor but two weeks since and had been assured there was no other like it . . . then, as the Prologue begins his piece again, pick up your stool and creep across the stage to the other side.

After some more chat and fidgeting, as soon as the actors appear:

take from your pocket tobacco, and your pipe and all the stuff belonging to it and make much of filling and lighting it. [Then, as the leading actor strides on to begin his great opening speech] comment loudly on his little legs, or his new hat, or his red beard. Take no notice of those who cry out 'Away with the fool!' It shall crown you with the richest commendation to laugh aloud in the midst of the most serious and saddest scenes of the terriblest tragedy and to let that clapper, your tongue, be tossed so high the whole house may ring with it. Lastly you shall disgrace the author of this piece worst, whether it is a comedy, pastoral or tragedy, if you rise with a screwed and discontented face and be gone. No matter whether the play be good or not, the better it is the more you should dislike it. Do not sneak away like a coward, but salute all your gentle acquaintance that are spread out either on the rushes or on the stools behind you, and draw what troop you can from the stage after you. The Poet may well cry out 'and a pox go with you!' but care not you for that; there's no music without frets.

So, with the feeling of a job well done, it is time for the evening meal. There is, however, one problem. By now there is no money to pay for it:

So you will need to find, to pay your reckoning for you, some young man lately come into his inheritance who is in London for the first time; a country gentleman who has brought his wife up to learn the fashions, see the tombs in Westminster, the lions in the Tower or to take physic; or else some farmer who has told his wife back home he has a suit at law and is come to town to pursue his lechery – for all these will have money in their purses and good conscience to spend it.

On entering the tavern, the young hopeful should call all the drawers (the bar staff) by their given names, Jack, Will or Tom, and ask them if they still attend the fencing or dancing school to which he recommended them. 'Then clip mine hostess firmly around the waist and kiss her heartily, so calling to the Boy "to fetch me my money from the bar", as if you had left some there, rather than that you owed it. Pretend the reckoning they give you is but an account of your funds. Aim to have the gulls tell each other "here is some grave gallant!"'

Having made his entrance, he should then make a show of visiting the kitchen to see what is being prepared, returning after a little while to recommend this or that dish before joining one of the innocent countrymen at his table and dining in:

as great a state as a churchwarden among his parishioners at Pentecost or Christmas. For your drink, let not your physician confine you to one particular liquor; for as it is required that a gentleman should not always be plodding away at one art, but rather be a general scholar (that is, to have a lick of all sorts of learning, then away), so it is not fitting a man should trouble his head with sucking at one grape, but that he may be able to drink *any* strange drink. . . . [At this stage, Dekker recommends] you should enquire which great gallants are supping in a private room then, whether or not you know them, send them up a bottle of wine saying that it is at your expense. Round off your meal by announcing to the whole room what a gallant fellow you are, how much you spend yearly in the taverns, what a gamester, what custom you bring to the house, in what witty discourse you maintain a table, what gentlewomen or citizens wives you can, at the crook of your finger, have at any time to sup with you – and such like.

This sort of behaviour should immensely impress the diners:

who will greatly admire you and think themselves in paradise but to be in your acquaintance. . . . After further such discourse and, possibly, a game or two of dice (which you must take care to win), and the time comes to leave, give your hostess a hearty kiss, down a last flagon, dowse your face with sweet water and when the terrible reckoning [bill] makes you hold up your hand and you must answer it at the bar, you must not abate one penny in any particular, no though they reckon beef to you when you have neither eaten, nor could ever abide it, rare or toasted. [Never argue over the bill for it makes you look] as if you were acquainted with the rates of the market.

After which, with one last flourish, you sweep off into the night leaving those you have entertained all evening to pay the bill.

Eventually it really is time to go home to bed. The street can be a dangerous place late at night, the haunt of thieves and cut-throats, so if you should run into some doubtful character then shout loudly, as if to your man, to hurry along or you'll 'pull his cap about his ears' in the morning. But there is, of course, the possibility that you might be taken for some kind of rogue or desperado yourself and should you therefore have the misfortune to run into the Watch, if you have with a friend with you:

address him loudly as 'Sir Giles' or 'Sir Abram'. . . . It matters not that there is no dubbed knight in your company, the Watch will wink at you for the love they bear to arms and knighthood. If you have no sweet mistress to whom you may retire, then continue speaking loudly how you and your shoal of gallants have swum through an ocean of wine, that you have danced out the heels of

your shoes and how happy you are to have paid all the reckoning
. . . that this may be published; the only danger in this is that if
you owe money, your creditors might get it by the ears which, if
they do, you will look to have a peal of ordnance thundering at
your chamber door in the morning demanding what you owe.
[Should such a misfortune occur, then] you should appear to them
in your nightshirt, clutching a glass in your hand and saying that
only today have you been purged of your terrible sickness . . . this
should drive them quickly back into their holes.

With that Dekker bids his protégé and the reader 'good night',
promising a whole lot more advice on the morrow 'but enough is
enough, at least for one night. Yet if, as I perceive you relish this first
lesson well, the rest I will prepare for you.'

Obviously Dekker was writing tongue-in-cheek – 'I sing like a
cuckoo in June to be laughed at' – but there is a good deal of truth
in it. Regarding the fashion for sitting at the side of the stage very
obviously smoking a pipe, we can return to Guilpin at the beginning
of this chapter:

> See you him yonder who sits o'er the stage,
> With the Tobacco pipe now at his mouth?
> It is Cornelius that brave gallant youth,
> Who is new printed to this fangled age,
> He wears a Jerkin cudgelled with gold lace,
> A profound slop, a hat scarce pipkin high.

As to bad behaviour in general, according to M.C. Bradbrook, in
1590 Richard Burbage, driven beyond endurance, grabbed a man
who made trouble in The Theatre, disrupting the performance, 'and
playing scornfully with this deponent's nose uttered threats of bodily
violence'.[3] Nor is it unlikely that playwrights such as Greene and
Dekker, who were always short of ready cash, were quite prepared
either to pretend to be other than they were or to play on their
known talent in exchange for a free meal.

FIVE

Performances, Plays and Politics

Defer not with me to this last point of extremity, for little
knowest thou how, in the end, thou shalt be visited.
Greene's *Groatsworth of Wit Bought with a Million of
Repentance* (1592)

The shadows were now deepening in Gloriana's England although
the climate of the times had been changing since the execution of
Mary, Queen of Scots, followed by the defeat of the Spanish Armada
in 1588. For the threat from Spain did not end with the vanquishing
of the Armada. From then until his death two years later, Sir Francis
Walsingham's intelligencers were continually telling him of
negotiations going on between factions in Ireland and the Spanish
government to land a Spanish force there, a matter of great concern
and one proved all too real during the later 1590s when two attempts
were made to do just that. No longer were Catholics allowed to get
on with their lives so long as they put in an appearance at church or
paid their fines for not doing so and anti-Catholicism in general was
on the rise. Nor did the Queen's refusal to name King James VI of
Scotland as her heir help, and throughout the decade of the 1590s
and up until her death in 1603 there were undercover
communications with Edinburgh both on a semi-official basis and by
those who sought to ingratiate themselves with the man who would
one day be their King. To add to the general feeling of unease the
plague, Nashe's 'King Pest', returned in 1592; the epidemic was to
last for well over a year but when the theatres were open audiences
flocked in to escape the reality of what was going on around them.

During the early 1590s they had a rich field of drama from which
to choose. The dating of plays has academics at each others' throats

60

not least because the date on which a play was registered at Stationer's Hall is no real guide, as often the registration did not take place until several years after its first performance even though it was one of the few ways a writer could attempt to protect his work. While there has never been copyright on ideas, unscrupulous dramatists were more than capable of sitting in on a public performance and making notes on the text. But in view of what was to come we know for certain that all Marlowe's plays had been written by May 1593 even if, apart from the two parts of *Tamburlaine*, there is disagreement as to the order in which this happened. Several sources however do suggest that his next play was *The Jew of Malta*, followed by *Edward II*, then *A Massacre at Paris* (of which only fragments remain) and finally *Dr. Faustus*.

The Jew of Malta proved extremely popular even if it was not as exciting as *Tamburlaine* with its great processions, magnificent court scenes and battles, not to mention the pampered jades of Asia. However the average Elizabethan was deeply suspicious of Jews, associating them with money-lending and worse, and considering them to be devious, cunning and untrustworthy. Therefore Barabas, the Jew of Malta, was bound to be a scoundrel. But Marlowe's play is not as simple as that. First he brings on to the stage an actor playing the part of a real historical person, Niccolo Machiavelli, considered wrongly by those who had heard of him as the epitome of evil rather than as the devious political pragmatist he actually was. But few in the audiences or beyond were likely to have read *The Prince* and both Barabas, and Shakespeare's Richard III, have been described ever since as 'machiavellian' villains.

We first meet Barabas checking out his great wealth in his counting house congratulating himself on the amount he has amassed. Almost immediately, however, he is attacked by Christian soldiers who seize his wealth and make off with it simply because he is a Jew. Not surprisingly he is determined to be revenged and we follow his progress to this end, and his playing off of Christians against Muslims, until he meets his death by being boiled in a cauldron. This was obviously the high spot of the afternoon's entertainment and 'a Cauldron for the Jew' appears prominently on one of Henslowe's lists of current props. There is a good deal of black humour in the play, not least the competitive exchange between Barabas and the Turk, Ithamore, as to who has carried out the most evil deeds and in which Barabas brags that he has sometimes 'gone about and poisoned wells', the device suggested to students at Douai. The Jew might be the obvious villain and the Christians supposedly the 'heroes', cheering to the echo as he boils away in his cauldron – but Marlowe, in a final twist, reveals that the only honourable men in the play are the Muslims, betrayed then murdered by those very Christians to whom they have offered the hand of friendship.

But it was *Edward II* that would raise the danger stakes for Marlowe. The source for his subject was Holinshed's *Chronicles*, his perspective on it his own. Plays about kings were now extremely popular but *Edward II* was quite unlike any previous play about a king or, for a very long time, any succeeding one, dealing as it does with the obsessive love of the King for two male favourites, especially the first, Piers Gaveston. Of recent years it has been generally accepted that Edward was homosexual (though it would seem from two new biographies that this is now open to question) but the extravagant affection and language used between Edward and Gaveston in Marlowe's play leaves one in little doubt as to what he thought, and the relationship between them is entirely believable. Marlowe's real difficulty is with Queen Isabella. He was simply unable to create credible female characters and she is no exception. In the first part of the play she is one of his usual lifeless women. In the second, by which time she has taken Mortimer as a lover and both are set to rebel against the King, she has turned without explanation into a two-dimensional harpy. Isabella is a thankless part for an actress. At the end of the play Edward meets his death in the dungeons of Berkeley Castle in the manner popularly accepted, and no doubt considered apposite by the average playgoer of the day – at the end of a red hot poker.

Although Alleyn doubtless gave a splendid performance in the title role, it never achieved the popularity of either *Tamburlaine*, *The Jew* or *Dr. Faustus*. Even today it remains a difficult role for an actor, who is faced with having to present Edward as deeply unsympathetic in the first half of the play, yet somehow has to gain our sympathy in the second, again without showing how he progresses from one to the other. Also, even today, some audiences seem to find it hard to take the overt exchanges of passion between Edward and Gaveston.

Dr. Faustus, however, was a different matter altogether. The legend of Faust was an old one but a new translation of *The Damnable Life and Deserved Death of Dr. Faustus* was published in 1592 and it immediately grabbed Marlowe's imagination. Marlowe, amoral, intellectually brilliant, fascinated by the 'new learning', driven by demons of his own and loving to shock, had found the perfect theme. The boast he gives to Faustus that 'this word damnation terrifies not me' might have applied just as well to the character's creator. The concept that man will do literally anything, including selling his own soul for power and forbidden knowledge, remains as potent as ever even in an age when there is no longer any widespread belief in Heaven and Hell. People who have never seen or read the play still know the meaning of the term 'Faustian bargain'.

Audiences were thrilled to the core. Here was the overreacher to end them all, a man prepared to sell his soul to Satan through his messenger, Mephistopheles, and sign the bargain in his own blood. Already they knew how it would end, of course – the excitement was in the anticipation. 'How comes it then that thou art out of hell?', enquires Faustus, to which his tempter responds, 'Why, this is hell, nor am I out of it'. It was obvious where Faustus was bound. So as well as following Faustus's progress to damnation and seeing him try out his supernatural powers, not least ordering up Helen of Troy as a tasty dish, the drama enabled the theatre to show off its most spectacular special effects. Turning to Henslowe once again, we know that the Rose Theatre boasted a huge 'Hell Mouth', and that at the end of the play Faustus was dragged down to Hell by a host of howling demons, most likely in a cloud of red smoke and to the rattle of thunder sheets.

Because of its subject matter, not to mention what soon befell its author, *Dr. Faustus* acquired something of the reputation that still

attaches to *Macbeth* today. So awful was the scale of Faustus's sin
that we are told that when Alleyn played the role he always wore a
cross around his neck and a surplice under his costume, just in case.
There are also tales of performances during which audiences were
convinced that they had seen 'the visible appearance of the Devil on
the stage'. A widely recorded account from Exeter states that:

> certain players acting upon the stage the tragical story of Dr.
> Faustus the Conjuror, as a certain number of devils kept everyone
> his circle there, and as Faustus was busy in his magical
> invocations, on a sudden they were all dashed, everyone
> harkening the other in the ear, for they were all persuaded that
> there was one devil too many among them. And so after a little
> pause desired the people to pardon them, they could go no further
> in this matter: the people also understanding the thing as it was,
> every man hastened to be first out of the doors. The players, as I
> heard it, contrary to their custom of spending the night in reading
> and in prayer, got them out of town the next morning.[1]

Meanwhile Shakespeare was rapidly becoming established as a
popular dramatist. Here too there is tremendous disagreement
among the experts as to what was written when but almost
certainly *Titus Andronicus*, *Two Gentlemen of Verona*, *Comedy of
Errors*, *The Taming of the Shrew* and *Richard III* were written and
performed between the years 1589 and 1594. Indeed opinion is
divided into two camps over *Comedy of Errors*, one putting its first
performance some time in 1589, the other in 1594. There is no
doubt that the play was in Burbage's repertoire by 1594 because of
a somewhat unfortunate incident or series of incidents leading to
the arrest of the cast. Burbage and his actors had been hired to
provide an entertainment for the law students at the Inns of Court.
There are no details as to what actually took place after the
performance, only that it resulted in a court case 'due to the great
disorders and abuses done and committed during the evening by a
company of base common fellows under the leadership of a sorcerer
or conjuror'.[2]

The plot, taken from the Roman author Plautus, concerns two sets of twins, each pair consisting of a master and his servant, who were parted shortly after their births. The master and servant of one pair find themselves in Ephesus where their counterparts have been living since they were children, with genuinely funny and confusing results. Adriana, the wife of the Ephesus twin, having taken the 'wrong' twin back home assuming it is her husband (and possibly spending the afternoon in bed with him) then finds his behaviour so inexplicable that she decides he must be mad and sends for a 'conjuror' to cast out his devils. Presumably it was the actor playing this part who was accused of causing mayhem. Whoever he was, he defended himself and his fellow-actors so well, accusing the attorney and solicitor who brought them to court of 'knavery and juggling' in presenting their case, that it was promptly dismissed.[3]

Commenting on the incident, one Henry Helmus noted that as an evening out the entertainment 'was not thought to offer much of account, save Dancing and Revelling with Gentlewomen and after such Sports a *Comedy of Errors*, like to Plautus his *Menechmus*, was played by the Players. So that the night was begun, and continued to the end, in nothing but confusion and errors, whereupon it was ever afterwards known as the Night of Errors.' He then adds: 'Gray's Inn Hall, Innocents Day, December 28 1594. There was such a row and such crowding by gentlewomen and others on the stage, that the Temple visitors to Gray's Inn went away disgusted. And so the Gray's Inn Men had only Dancing and Shakespeare's Play.'

The Shrew needs little or no explanation and was likely based on an older, existing drama on the same subject; *Titus Andronicus* is a blood-stained tale of murder and rape which culminates with children being eaten in a pie, while *Two Gentlemen* is a gentle comedy which introduces one of Shakespeare's favourite themes where a boy player, dressed as a girl, disguises him/herself as a boy. As for *Richard III*, after *Spanish Tragedy*, it remained the most popular play in repertoire through until the end of the decade and no less than six editions of it were published in Shakespeare's lifetime. It offered the audience everything: a supposedly machiavellian villain who takes the audience into his confidence from the start, love (or lust) with the widow across the coffin of her husband whom he has only recently killed, executions and murders galore, hauntings by ghosts and an all-out battle scene at the end in which the protagonist almost redeems himself by his outstanding courage. For Elizabethans it was important to have 'a good death'.

This play too acquired a mythology of its own, including the famous tale which appears in the *Diary* of John Manningham, a student at the Middle Temple, in the year 1602:

> Upon a time when Burbage played Richard III there was a female citizen grew so far in liking with him, that before she went from the play she appointed him to come that night unto her by the name Richard III. Shakespeare, overhearing their conclusion, went before, was entertained, and at his game ere Burbage came. The message being brought that Richard III was at the door, Shakespeare caused the return to be made that William the Conqueror was before Richard III.[4]

True or not it gives a good idea of what actors and dramatists were up to when the opportunity arose.

Another reason for the change in the climate of the times, which bred general suspicion and unease, was the death of Sir Francis Walsingham. His demise resulted in a major political vacancy, that of Secretary of State to the Privy Council, bringing with it the role of spymaster. It was a position which had been coveted by Lord Burleigh's son, Sir Robert Cecil, for many years, and his father, as Elizabeth's oldest and most trusted minister, did all he could to ensure his son achieved it, which he did in all but name. However, for whatever reason Elizabeth showed little enthusiasm for making his position official with the result that Cecil was the 'acting' Secretary of State (unpaid) for the next seven years. No doubt the Queen saw this as a useful economy.

It was during the winter of 1591/2 that the first signs of plague began to appear. There was scarcely a year without a handful of cases, but this was to prove an epidemic of appalling proportions, killing 10,675 people before it finally ran its course. Almost at once the government ordered the closure of theatres and other public places where people gathered, as a result of which the Rose Theatre was shut from February until the following Christmas; this forced the players, faced with the prospect of having no income at all, to go on the road. Alleyn headed a company made up of actors from several London companies which toured under the name of Lord Strange's Men. In spite of it being such a gloomy spring, Alleyn had married Henslowe's stepdaughter, Joan Woodward, thus bringing about, as one commentator has it, 'Henslow-Alleyn theatrical enterprises'. While it might have been very useful for Alleyn to stitch himself into the Henslowe family, his letters to Joan when out on tour also show a true and genuine affection for her.

However neither the onset of the plague nor his monarch's obvious lack of enthusiasm in any way diminished Sir Robert Cecil's zeal for the job in hand, whether or not his position had been officially confirmed. While Walsingham was a clever politician who could when necessary be quite ruthless, Cecil was an even less sympathetic character. Clever, cold, calculating and in both senses of the word truly Machiavellian, he saw the internal security of the country as his top priority. His intelligencers were everywhere. Jesuit priests were hunted down with ruthless efficiency and when found were tortured before being hanged, drawn and quartered. Those whose loyalty was only mildly questionable, or who were thought to be making overtures to King James in Edinburgh as they looked to their future, were put under the sixteenth-century equivalent of surveillance. The atmosphere became increasingly one of unease and suspicion bordering on paranoia.

It is therefore not surprising that Marlowe's increasingly reckless behaviour was beginning to draw the attention of the authorities. His first real clash with the law had occurred as far back as 1589 and it was by no means all his fault. The report of the subsequent inquest held in September 1589 on one William Bradley, 'lying dead and slain of a wound, six inches in depth and one inch in breadth, in the right side of his chest', records the results of a fatal sword fight.[5] Bradley, a quarrelsome young man prone to easy violence, was the son of an innkeeper in Gray's Inn Lane and had been in a long-running quarrel with Marlowe's friend and fellow university wit, Thomas Watson. Marlowe had probably first met Watson through Thomas Walsingham, for Watson had been in Paris in 1581 when Walsingham's uncle, Sir Francis, was spending some time there. Apparently Sir Francis admired Watson's poetry and his 'tunes', or madrigals, and encouraged him to have his work published, which he did to considerable acclaim. Music remained a great love and as well as the poets and dramatists, he numbered composers like William Byrd among his friends. His background was, however, an odd one for while he appears to have studied Law in Italy, he is also said to have spent time in the English College at Douai, although it has never been suggested that he, like Marlowe, was acting as an intelligencer.

The original quarrel between Bradley and Watson had arisen over a debt of £14 owed by Bradley to another innkeeper, John Alleyn, brother of the famous actor. Bradley ignored all John Alleyn's attempts to get him to repay his debt, even when Alleyn threatened him with court action to be brought through his lawyer, Hugh Swift. Bradley's reaction was akin to something out of the long-running soap opera, *EastEnders*: he threatened to send a heavy mob round to Swift to see to him if he dared take the matter to court. Swift appealed to the Queen's Bench for 'securities of the peace', which was granted and the matter continued to rumble on. Swift's brother-in-law was no other than Thomas Watson and in spite of their appeal to the Bench being granted, Bradley's threats had reached the point where Watson and John Alleyn decided to take the matter into their own hands and sort Bradley out themselves, resulting in Bradley in turn appealing to the Bench for securities of the peace. So, for a while, there was stalemate until Bradley, who had somehow decided that all his troubles were down to Watson in the first place, buckled on his rapier and dagger and set off to settle the matter once and for all.

He made his way to Norton Folgate where both Watson and Marlowe lodged, and lurked around waiting for his quarry. But as time passed and there was no sign of Watson, Bradley went looking for him in nearby Hog Lane. So it was that by fatal chance he came across Marlowe, whom he knew to be Watson's friend and whom he then publicly and loudly insulted. What he said is not recorded – though it might be imagined since Marlowe made no secret of his proclivities – but the result was that Marlowe promptly drew his sword and challenged him to fight; an exciting piece of entertainment for passers-by who no doubt stood cheering them on. It is clear that Marlowe, no mean fighter, would have taken the engagement to its ultimate conclusion but at that point Watson himself turned up, whereupon Bradley called out 'art thou now come, then I will have a bout with thee' and turned his attention to his real enemy, leaving Marlowe with no option but to step aside.

The subsequent fight moved up and down Hog Lane, the combatants using both rapier and dagger, until Bradley drove Watson, now bleeding from a wound, to a ditch at the north end where, with nowhere else to run, he turned and thrust his rapier home, running Bradley badly through. He died almost at once. By this time someone had gone to fetch the Constable who immediately took Watson and Marlowe before the local Justice of the Peace, Sir Owen Hopton, who drew up a warrant 'on suspicion of murder' and had them both taken to Newgate prison.

As was the custom, the inquest on Bradley was held the next day before the Middlesex coroner, Ian Chalkhill. The twelve-man jury, after hearing all the evidence, concluded that Watson slew Bradley in self-defence and 'not by felony'. That being the case Watson and Marlowe must have expected to be set free almost immediately but they remained in Newgate even though Marlowe had not actually struck the fatal blow. He finally managed to get himself out on bail a couple of weeks later bound over to attend the next Sessions on 3 December, but poor Watson languished in Newgate for no good reason until 12 February 1590, by which time he was a sick man as his wound had become infected.

There is a strong possibility that the intelligencer, Robert Poley, witnessed the fight since he lived nearby at the time and it has been said that Shakespeare who, if he did not actually see it, most certainly would have heard about it, used the incident of a three-cornered sword-fight in *Romeo and Juliet*. It is also suggested that the character of Mercutio was based on Marlowe.

Perhaps now is the time to introduce another character to the London scene, one Dr Gabriel Harvey, the eldest son of a wealthy Essex rope-maker, described by Nashe as 'the Harveys of Hemp Hall'.[6] After graduating at Christ's College, he had become first a Fellow of Pembroke Hall, then a Trinity Fellow where he studied Civil Law. He was considered an excellent scholar destined for greatness; he had a powerful patron, the Earl of Leicester, while his friends included Spenser and Sidney. But that was as good as it was going to get for so certain was he that he was indeed destined for greatness, he became notorious for his pomposity, grandiose behaviour and overwhelming conceit. In fact he appears to have been a gentleman version of Shakespeare's Malvolio who also expected greatness to be 'thrust upon' him.

He had no time whatsoever for the University Wits and wrote scathingly even of the respectable John Lyly, whom he saw as 'an odd, light-headed fellow . . . a professed jester, a Hick-scorner, a scoff-master, a playmonger, an Interluder; once the foil of Oxford, now the stale of London, and ever the Apesclogg of the press'. Needless to say the objects of his dislike paid him back in kind. Nashe describes how he went abroad of an evening 'holding his gown up to his middle, that the wenches may see what a fine leg and a dainty foot he hath', a 'mere lute-pin put in a suit of apparel'. But Harvey too would have a role to play before the end of 1593.

On 9 May Marlowe was once again in trouble with the law. He had been drinking heavily, nothing unusual by then. Nor was there anything unexpected about the effect it had on him and his subsequent behaviour after several hours on the wine or sack. Roaring back towards his lodgings, he (literally) ran into Allen Nicholls, constable of Shoreditch, who was walking the other way with his assistant constable, Nicholas Helliot. What happened next depends on who tells the story – whether Marlowe merely behaved aggressively and failed to apologise or actually took a swing at Nicholls – but either way he ended up in court brought before no other justice than that very same Sir Owen Hopton who had presided over his previous court appearance after Bradley's death.[7]

Obviously this was nothing like so serious a charge but even famous poets and dramatists cannot be allowed to get away with insulting the authorities. He was fined the sum of £20, no small amount in 1592, and released:

> Upon Condition that he will personally appear at the next general Session of the peace held in and for the aforesaid county [Middlesex]: and meanwhile will keep the peace towards the whole people of the said lady Queen Elizabeth and especially towards Allen Nicholls, Constable of Hollowwell street in the aforesaid county, and Nicholas Helliot, underconstable of the same; Which sum aforesaid he permits to be raised for the use of the said lady Queen in the form of a Recognizance from his goods, chattels, land and tenements, if he should fail in his promise.

In other words Marlowe had been bound over to keep the peace. There is no doubt that he often caused offence, indeed almost took pride in it. In so many ways he is a very modern figure, the boy from the sticks, born into a humble background who, through his own undoubted talent, soars to the top of his profession, achieves fame and adulation, becomes over-arrogant, drinks far too much and heads toward disaster.

The number of plague victims was growing inexorably. Alleyn, out on tour and increasingly worried, wrote to Joan, his 'Mouse':

> I commend me heartily to you, and to my father and my mother and my sister, Bess, hoping in God though the sickness be round about you, yet by his mercy it may escape your house, which by the grace of God it shall. Therefore use this course: keep your house fair and clean, which I know you will, and every evening throw water before your door and in your back side, and have in your windows good store of rue and herb of grace, and with all the grace of God, which must be obtained by prayers and so doing, no doubt but that the Lord will mercifully defend you.[8]

Henslowe replied on Joan's behalf, possibly because she was illiterate, saying that she prayed day and night for his good health and 'hoping in the Lord Jesus that we shall have again a merry meeting; for I have been flyted with fear of sickness, but thanks be unto God we are all at this time in good health in our house. But all round about us it hath been almost in every house, and whole households are dead. . . . There hath died this last week 1,603 . . . which has been the greatest that came yet.' Among them was the entire family of one of his actors, Robert Browne. 'Robert Browne's wife in Shoreditch and all her children and household be dead, and her doors shut up.'

Many people, not least most of the physicians, fled London for the safety of the country – a point made somewhat acidly in his diary by Dr Forman. He had contracted the plague himself in April and 'cured' himself of it. In fairness, once he had recovered, he worked tirelessly among the sick going into houses where no other doctor would venture, to do what he could for the victims.[9] As is always the case there were those too who saw it as a way of making a quick guinea. One such was Simon Kellaway who published a *Defensative Against the Plague*, which lists a number of supposed prophylactics. Customers buying his pamphlet to find out how they might save their lives were informed that the most effective method was '*fugi locis*'. Those unable to read Latin had to have it translated only to discover they had paid good money to be told to 'flee the place'.

Robert Greene, meanwhile, had parted from Emma Ball and was now living as indigent as ever in lodgings with a cobbler and his wife. He had walked out on Emma when she was pregnant, leaving her to give birth to a sickly baby which she was now struggling to rear and to whom she had given the unsuitable name of Fortunatus. She no longer had any support from her brother either, for Cutting Ball Jack had finally paid the price for his activities – on the scaffold at Tyburn, an execution which had drawn large crowds.

In spite of having no money, Greene kept up his dissolute lifestyle, causing Gabriel Harvey to deliver one of his all-too-frequent homilies:

Who in London has not heard of his dissolute and licentious living; his fond disguising of a Master of Arts with ruffianly hair, unseemly apparel, and more unseemly company; his vainglorious and Thrasonical bragging; his piperly extemporising and Tarletonising; his apish counterfeiting of every ridiculous and absurd toy; his villainous cogging and foisting; his monstrous swearing and horrible forswearing; his impious profaning of sacred texts; his other riotous and outrageous surfeitings; his continual shifting of lodgings; his plausible mustering, and banqueting of roisterly acquaintance at his first coming; his beggarly departure in every hostess's debt; his infamous resorting to the Bankside, Shoreditch, Southwark and other filthy haunts; his obscure lurking in the basest corners; his pawning of his sword, cloak and what not, when money came short; his impudent pamphleteering, fantastical interluding and desperate libelling; when other cozening shifts failed; his employing Ball (known as Cutting Ball), 'til he was intercepted at Tyburn, to lend a crew of his trustiest companions to guard him in danger of arrest; his keeping of the aforesaid Ball's sister, a sorry ragged quean, of whom he has had a base born son, *In*fortunatus Greene; his forsaking of his own wife, too honest for such a husband. Particulars are infinite: his condemning of his superiors, deriding of others, and defying all good order?[10]

Needless to say Greene responded in kind, insulting Harvey's father as a mere 'halter-maker', following this up with scandalous gossip about his brothers, alleging that the eldest, although he was a parson, chased after his parishioners' wives, that the second was a fool who dabbled in astrology, while the third, supposedly given to academic study, had recently been 'clapped in the Fleet Prison'. Yet most of those who knew Greene had a soft spot for him, however appalling his behaviour, among them Henry Chettle who published the works of a number of dramatists including those of Greene. He described the poet/playwright at this time as 'a man of indifferent years' (actually he was thirty-five), 'of face amiable, of body well proportioned, his attire after the habit of a gentleman, only his hair is somewhat long'.

But throughout that plague-ridden summer, Greene was becoming increasingly ill due, most likely, to years of heavy drinking added to past venereal infections, and by the end of it he was no longer writing plays or 'Interludes'. By mid-August it was clear that he was dying, hounded to the end by his creditors and pursued by Harvey who was threatening to sue him for defamation of character. As death drew ever nearer, Greene became terrified of what was to come and, fearful of damnation, produced two pamphlets warning others of his fate, his *Groatsworth of Wit Bought with a Million of Repentance* and *The Repentance of Robert Greene* in which he turned his venom on his friends and the players and writers among whom he had lived and worked for so many years.

His view of Shakespeare is well known:

> for unto none of you, like me, sought these burrs (actors) to cleave; those puppets, I mean, that spake from our mouths, those antics garnished in our colours. Is it not strange that I, to whom they have all been beholding, shall – were that ye were in that case as I am now – be both at once of them forsaken? Yea, trust them not; for there is an upstart crow, beautified with our feathers, that with his 'Tiger's heart wrapped in a Player's hide', supposes he is well able to bombast out blank verse as the best of you, and being an absolute Johannes Factotum is, in his own conceit, the only Shake-Scene in the country.

The lad from Warwickshire had never been truly accepted by the University Wits.

In fact by this time Shakespeare must already have become a highly respected dramatist, for the printer, Henry Chettle, who had published Greene's *Groatsworth of Wit*, wrote later that two of those mentioned in it had taken offence:

> About three months since died M. Robert Greene, leaving many papers in sundry booksellers' hands, among them his *Groatsworth of Wit*, in which a letter, written to diverse playmakers is offensively by one or two of them taken; and because on the dead

they cannot be avenged, they wilfully forge in their conceits a living author; and after tossing it to and fro, no remedy but it must light on me. How I have all the time of my conversing in printing scholars, it hath been very well known; and how on that I dealt, I can sufficiently prove. With neither of them that take offence was I acquainted, and with one of them I care not if I never be. The other, whom at that time I did not so much spare as since I wish I had, for that, as I have moderated in the heat of living writers, and might have used my own discretion – especially in such a case, the author being dead – that I am not as sorry as if the original fault had been my fault, because myself have seen his demeanour no less civil, than he excellent in the qualities he professes; – besides, divers of worship have reported his uprightness and his facetious grace in writing, that approves his art.[11]

Which, all in all, is quite a testimonial. For Marlowe, so long his rival in the theatre and close companion in drink, roistering and the enjoyment of the low life, there is now only condemnation, especially of his 'unnatural vice'. His final warning to his old friend echoes down the centuries with a prescient and chilling resonance: 'I know the least of my demerits merit this miserable death but wilful striving against known truth exceedeth all the terrors of my soul. Defer not with me till this last point of extremity, for little knowest thou how, in the end, thou shalt be visited.'

Marlowe was to suffer a double blow as Tom Watson died at about the same time as Greene, probably of the plague. Watson was one of his greatest and most loyal friends. There is no date recorded for his death but given the scale of the epidemic that is hardly surprising, for Thomas Dekker records how plague victims of all degrees and ages were tumbled anonymously into the plague pits at dead of night, regardless of rank, age or sex.

Greene staged his own deathbed as theatrically as he had everything else in his short life, complaining loudly to those gathered around him that he was dying only as a result of eating too many pickled herrings washed down with Rhenish wine. To the end he behaved particularly unkindly to Emma Ball who came to see him, bringing the baby with her, to beg him to recognise little Fortunatus as his son but he refused to do so, sending her away without a kind word. Finally, aware that time was running out, he sent for paper and ink and wrote to his long-estranged wife, 'from whose sight and company I have refrained these six years: I ask God and thee forgiveness for so greatly wronging thee, of whom I seldom or never thought until now. Pardon me, I pray you, wheresoever thou art, and God forgive me all my other offences.' He then added: 'Sweet Wife, as ever there was goodwill or friendship between thee and me, see this bearer (my Host) satisfied of his debt. I owe him ten pounds and but for him, I had perished in the streets. Forget and forgive my wrongs done to thee, and Almighty God have mercy on my soul. Farewell till we meet again in heaven, for on earth thou shall never see me more. This second of September 1592. Written by thy dying husband, Robin Greene.' He died the next day.

At the first whiff that the illness was fatal, Gabriel Harvey was knocking on the doors of Greene's neighbours eager to learn all the gory details of his last days. Finally, hearing that 'Greene had played his last part and gone to Tarlton', he went directly to Greene's landlady, who met him 'with tears in her eyes and sighs from a deeper fountain (for she loved him dearly) and told me of his lamentable begging of a penny-pot of Malmsey . . .'. He then added, nastily and most likely untruthfully, that Greene's only deathbed visitors had been two women, 'Emma Ball, sister to the rogue, Cutting Ball lately hanged at Tyburn, demanding a name for her bastard, and a woman associate'.

However, in spite of Harvey's bitching, tradition has it that Greene was buried in style, accompanied to his grave by his fellow writers, his corpse strewn by his landlady with garlands of bay as befitted a poet. The anonymous R.B. in Greene's *Funerals*, published in 1594 writes:

> Greene is the pleasing object of an eye:
> Greene pleased the eyes of all that looked on him.
> Greene is the ground of every painter's dye:
> Greene gave ground to all that wrote upon him,
> Nay more, the men that so eclipsed his fame
> Purloin his plumes: can they deny the same?

SIX

The Reckoning

Quod me Nutrit me Destruit.
(That which Nourishes me Destroys me)
> Latin inscription on the portrait
> thought to be that of Christopher Marlowe

The young man in the portrait stares out at us with dark, knowing eyes that are older than his years. His hair is long and he has a moustache and a small beard. He is obviously wearing his best clothes, a fashionably slashed black doublet with a fine gauze collar over that of his shirt. Even if we did not know who it might be, it is very striking.

That the portrait still exists is remarkable. In 1953 some workmen were making repairs to the Master's Lodge at Corpus Christi College. Rubble, old plaster and pieces of wood were still in a heap outside as it had been raining for several days and it had remained uncollected when an undergraduate, who was walking by, just happened to see something sticking out of the rubbish and investigated further. It turned out to be one of two broken wooden panels. He took them out to discover that on the reverse side of the panels was a portrait of a young man in an Elizabethan doublet. The undergraduate took his find to the librarian who put the two pieces together, had it photographed, then sent it to the National Portrait Gallery to see if they might have any idea who it might be. After close examination the Gallery told the librarian that it was definitely an Elizabethan painting but they had no idea who the subject was. Since the portrait was in very poor condition it was then sent away to experts for restoration.

So why should it be Marlowe? It is dated 1585 when the subject was twenty-one years of age, which Marlowe would have been in the year he took his BA after his work as an intelligencer. The young man in the picture must have been a Corpus Christi student, otherwise it is unlikely that the picture would have been kept in the Master's Lodge, where it must previously have been, hidden away somewhere, since it was found among the rubble from the renovations. Then there is the 'motto' or title on the left-hand side of the picture which could hardly be more apposite to what we know of Marlowe. It is not a well-known Latin tag of the day and has not been found anywhere else. The question is, why should Marlowe merit a portrait when there were far more important and wealthy students up at the same time? He was, after all, only a scholarship boy and still had his way to make as a poet and dramatist. The jury remains out and all one can say is that it looks like the Marlowe of one's imagination.

In less fraught and difficult times theatre would simply have grown and evolved as new writers came on to the scene without dramatists having to fear for their lives, although no doubt the authorities would always have kept an eye on what was going on, given the conservative view of the subversive nature of what went on in playhouses. Heavens, no one knew what ideas such stuff might encourage in the groundlings! Even so, given his lifestyle, Greene is still likely to have died as he did at the age he did and, given also the prevalence of epidemics and casual violence, it is quite possible Marlowe and Kyd would never have seen old age anyway. But it was a combination of events – the continuing presence of the plague throughout 1593, the deeply paranoid political climate and an influx of refugees from religious persecution on the continent seeking asylum – which was to prove fatal for Kyd and Marlowe.

Partly to escape the plague and also because it was a pleasant and comfortable place in which to write, Marlowe was spending a good deal of time at Thomas Walsingham's great house, Scadbury Manor in Kent, possibly still working on *Faustus* while contemplating his long poem, *Hero and Leander*. At some point that autumn he was called down to Canterbury on a family matter where, presumably after he had again been drinking heavily, he was involved in a fight with a local tailor in the Chequers Inn, during which he pulled a knife. He was arrested by the constable, put in the town gaol for the night, then brought up before the local justice and fined. Possibly a weakness for alcohol ran in the family for at least one of his sisters too had what we might describe as a 'drink problem'.

It also seems likely, if not certain, that with such a questing mind and a thirst for new knowledge, he had become a member of the circle which has become known as 'the School of the Night' and which met under the auspices of Sir Walter Ralegh at his London home. Its membership fluctuated and those involved did not advertise the fact that they belonged to it but we know, from the subsequent inquiry set up by Sir Robert Cecil, that its known members included Henry Percy, Earl of Northumberland, nicknamed 'the Wizard Earl', the great mathematician and astronomer Thomas Hariot, the geographer Robert Hues, William Warner, another mathematician and also an alchemist, and Emery Molyneux, globemaker, and friend and patron to Simon Forman, and a member of the powerful and influential Carey family, Sir George Carey. On the arts side there were the poets George Chapman and Matthew Roydon. What is certain is that Marlowe was a friend of Hariot and associated with Ralegh with whom he was on versifying terms.[1]

Marlowe's poem, 'The Passionate Shepherd to His Love', was very popular and recited and sung everywhere. In it the rustic wooer lists to the object of his affection the delights of the rural life that would be theirs if she would only come away and live with him; pleasures such as listening to birds singing madrigals, lying on beds of roses, she gowned in fine wool clasped about with coral and ivy buds, while in idyllic weather shepherds dance and sing the days away. It ends:

> The shepherds, swains shall dance and sing,
> For thy delight each May morning,
> If these delights thy mind may move,
> Then live with me, and be my love.

To which Ralegh had replied verse for verse in 'The Nymph's Reply to the Shepherd', pouring cold water and mocking the whole notion:

But Time drives flocks from field to fold;
When rivers rage and rocks grow cold;
And Philomel becometh dumb;
The rest complains of cares to come.
But could youth last, and love still breed,
Had joys no date, nor age no need,
Then these delights my mind might move,
To live with thee and be thy love.

It is hardly surprising, given the political climate, that a group or society which met under the leadership of a high profile person such as Ralegh to investigate and discuss subjects proscribed by the university curricula of the day became the object of rumour and speculation, and that its activities were drawn to the attention of Cecil. While Ralegh remained one of the Queen's great favourites he was obviously reluctant to make any move but Ralegh's clandestine marriage in 1592 to Elizabeth Throckmorton, one of Elizabeth's ladies-in-waiting, had earned him a stretch in the Tower and he no longer enjoyed his previous power at Court, so leaving vulnerable those associated with him. There are a number of reasons why Marlowe might have been singled out for surveillance and possibly his association with Ralegh's circle was one of them, but whatever the reasoning behind it, a government intelligencer and informer of the name of Richard Baines was employed to make a note of what he did and said.

Spring 1593 came to a tense and uneasy London where fear of the plague and general dissatisfaction was compounded by the growing number of asylum seekers from France and the Low Countries fleeing possible massacre or death at the stake. It is with a sense of *déjà vu* that one reads the accounts of the time. Far from welcoming fellow Protestants and offering them refuge, the reverse was the case. In spite of the fact that the majority of them were artisans capable of earning a living who would not therefore be a charge on the state, they were accused of forcing taxes to be raised, taking away honest employment from others, turning to crime, stealing wives and daughters and, last but not least, bringing in even more cases of plague. Therefore they should be sent back at once to where they came from. Graffiti to that effect was painted on walls, along with flyposting of an unpleasant verse:

> You strangers that inhabit this land
> Note this same writing, do it understand,
> Conceive it well for safeguard of your lives,
> Your goods, your children and your dearest wives.

The matter was discussed at Westminster when a new Bill 'against Alien Strangers selling by way of Retail any Commodities' was up for discussion and, as predictably as today, speakers in the subsequent debate took opposing sides. Several Honourable Members did object to the way asylum seekers were being spoken of and treated. 'This Bill should be ill for London, for the riches and renown of the City cometh by entertaining of Strangers and giving liberty unto them', said Sir John Wolley, while a Master Fuller added 'the exclamations of the City are exceeding pitiful and great against these Strangers who had not quiet times in their own countries', otherwise they would have returned home of their own accord. Master Finch took the well-known political fence-sitting view that 'we ought not to be uncharitable, but this must be the Rule. None must so relieve Strangers as to beggar themselves.' Others straight-forwardly opposed any notion of welcome or charity and wanted them deported without further delay.

Presumably it was the topicality of the issue that prompted a group of writers to unearth an old play dealing with episodes in the life of Sir Thomas More, which included scenes detailing a past insurrection following an influx of refugees into the country seeking sanctuary. At least six people originally had an input into the script, and academics have identified the hands of Thomas Kyd, Thomas Dekker, George Chapman, Thomas Heywood (who was to become a popular dramatist himself), Henry Chettle and Anthony Mundy. Once it was knocked into some sort of shape it was sent off to Sir Edward Tylney, Master of the Revels, for his approval and the necessary licence. Its authors obviously hoped that the theatres would soon reopen but even if this was not the case at least the play could be taken out on tour.

But Tylney did not like the script and it was returned with a note to the effect that no licence for its performance would be issued until substantial alterations had been made. On it Tylney had written 'leave out the insurrection wholly and the cause thereof and begin with Sir Tho. Moore at the Mayor's Sessions with a report afterwards of his good service done, being Sheriff of London, upon a mutiny against the Lombards only by a short report, and not otherwise at your own perils'. There were repeated marginal notes too objecting to the word 'strangers', demanding that the writers 'mend this', and whole scenes were crossed out. Some sources also suggest that Tylney was so concerned about the content of the play that he submitted the names of its authors to the Privy Council.[2]

Faced with this, yet another writer was called in. His identity remains a mystery, but because of the quality of the three folio pages he inserted in the text both Marlowe and Shakespeare have been suggested.[3] The insurrection scene was removed and the insertion put in its place, a piece of writing as relevant today as when it was written. More, faced with overwhelming prejudice against Flemish refugees, the 'strangers' in question, is given the words:

> . . . you'll put down strangers?
> Kill them, cut their throats, possess their houses,
> And lead the majesty of law in liam (leash),
> To slip him like a hound?

Suppose those opposing their presence in the country were, in turn, to become refugees, to which country would they flee?

> Go you to France or Flanders,
> To any German province, to Spain or Portugal,
> Nay anywhere that not adheres to England,
> Why, you must needs be strangers: would you be pleased
> To find a nation of such barbarous temper,

That breaking out in hideous violence,
Would not afford you an abode on earth?

The problem of the contemporary asylum seekers refused to go away. On 22 April 1593, following further public protests against them, a 'printed libel' was circulated, a bitter attack on Belgian, French and Dutch immigrants and other 'Strangers' living in London in which, in the name of 'the workers', they were threatened with severe beatings or worse at the hands of bands of apprentices and journeymen and given until 9 July to flee the country or else. Copies of this and other petitions currently circulating came to the attention of the Privy Council and they acted almost at once, publishing an Order to the effect that the publishing and circulating of such malicious libels must cease forthwith and that anyone found so doing would be punished with the utmost severity. In order to hunt down such persons and bring them to justice, law officers would, from now on, be entitled to search the house, workplace or lodgings of anyone suspected of this or similar crimes. Should there be any cause, however slight, to think that such a person had been discovered, then they must be arrested.

It ends on a chilling note: '. . . and after you shall have examined this person, if you shall find them to be suspected and they shall refuse to confess the truth, you shall, by the authority hereof, put them to the torture in Bridewell and by the extremity therefore, draw them to discover the knowledge they have. We pray you use your utmost travail and endeavour.' Torture aside, the rest of the Order appears a worthy response to the plight of an unfortunate minority. However, it also gave those employed by the Privy Council the freedom to enter anyone's house on the pretext of searching for malicious libels and Cecil was to use it.

By late April, although the plague was now fast abating, the theatres were still closed and Alleyn was again out on tour; on 2 May he wrote from Chelmsford to his 'good sweetheart and loving mouse', teasing her about the gossip that had reached him as to the part she played the previous day in the festivities greeting the beginning of May, when you were, by my Lord Mayor's officer, made to ride in a cart (in the procession), you and all your fellows. I am sorry to hear that those supporters, your strong legs, would not carry you away but let you fall into the hands of such termagants, but, mouse, when I come home, I'll be revenged on them, till when, mouse I bid thee farewell and prithee send me word how thou dost, and so my hearty commendations to my father, mother and sister, and so sweetheart the lord bless thee – from Chelmsford the 2nd day of May 1593, thine and nobody else's by God of Heaven, Edward Alleyn. Farewell mouse.[4]

This at least suggests that in some ways London was finally beginning to return to normal.

In early May, Marlowe was at Scadbury again. This was no doubt a relief to his friends for his behaviour was becoming increasingly wild. If he was aware that he was being watched (which he might well have been), then he made no attempt to curb what he did or said and with his tongue loosened by heavy drinking he is alleged to have said a great deal. It was almost as if he had programmed himself to self-destruct. Meanwhile Kyd was working away, very likely on the script of the More play so that it could be returned to the Master of the Revels. Certainly it was hoped that this time it would be passed for performance since, as well as Kyd's marginal notes, there are others suggesting possible casting. Fortune was finally about to smile on him. He told those who knew him that he had at last acquired a patron although he did not reveal who it was. It has been suggested that it was Lord Strange, Earl of Derby, which is quite likely since he had a company of players of his own. Certainly he could have had no idea that the sky was about to fall in on him.

We are unlikely ever to know why the authorities finally decided to move against Marlowe when they did but on 12 May, without warning, a number of officers burst open the door to the room where Kyd was working, flourishing a warrant to turn over his room and search for – what? Publications of Malicious Libels, he was told in answer to his query; the officers were acting under the terms of the Order. But why Kyd, the most inoffensive,

Ben Jonson, 1617.
(Portrait by Abraham van
Blyenberch. National
Portrait Gallery, London)

The putative portrait of
Christopher Marlowe.
(Reproduced by
permission of the Master
and Fellows of Corpus
Christi College, Cambridge)

Edward Alleyn, artist unknown.
(By permission of the Trustees of
Dulwich Picture Gallery)

Edward Alleyn in the role of Tamburlaine.
(From *A General Historie of the
Turkes*, 1597)

Richard Burbage. Possibly a self-
portrait. (By permission of the
Trustees of Dulwich Picture Gallery)

George Chapman. (Frontispiece to
a collection of the plays, Mermaid
Series, 1887)

John Fletcher. (Private Collection: Photographic Survey, Courtauld Institute of Art)

Right: Francis Beaumont. (From a frontispiece to a collection of the works of Beaumont and Fletcher, Mermaid Series, 1887)

Left: Gabriel Harvey, woodcut portrait, 1596

Thomas Middleton. (From the frontispiece to his plays, Mermaid Series, 1883)

The ghost of Robert Greene, woodcut, 1598.

Thomas Nashe, woodcut, 1597.

The great sixteenth-century clown Richard Tarlton, with pipe and tabor.

William Kempe pictured dancing his famous 'Jig' to Norwich, 1600.

Mary or 'Moll Frith':
the Roaring Girl.

Inside the Red Bull Playhouse. (From the
frontispiece to *Kirkman's Drolls*, 1672)

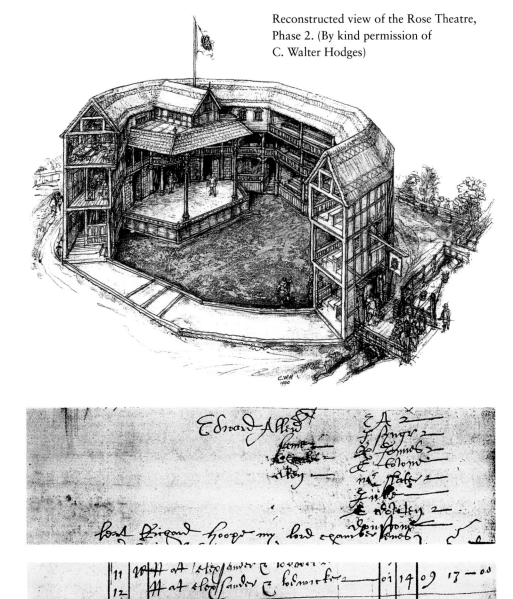

Reconstructed view of the Rose Theatre, Phase 2. (By kind permission of C. Walter Hodges)

Centre and bottom: From Henslowe's Diary: *Above,* List of Sharers of the Lord Admiral's Men, showing Edward Alleyn's signature. *Below,* Part of accounts page for March 1597. (By kind permission of Dulwich College)

Johannes de Witt's sketch of the Swan Theatre stage, 1596.

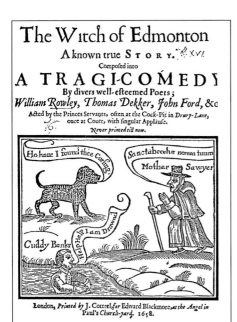

The Witch of Edmonton
Dekker, Ford and Rowley

A Game at Chess
Thomas Middleton

The Spanish Tragedy
Thomas Kyd

The Maid's Tragedy
Beaumont and Fletcher

A selection of Jacobean playbills.

unremarkable and respectable of all the dramatists who, apart from the success of *Spanish Tragedy*, had made no name for himself and still worked at his old trade of scrivener? It is highly unlikely that he could seriously have been suspected of publishing such stuff. But that was not what the officers were looking for. Apparently they knew that some eighteen months previously Marlowe, when he was in London, had shared the room with Kyd, using it as a much-needed place in which to work, an essential in the overcrowded noisy London of the day where privacy was a luxury afforded only to the wealthy. It did not take them long to find something incriminating: a pamphlet, considered heretical, written half a century earlier by a man called Arius.

Kyd protested that the pamphlet was nothing to do with him but one of a number of old papers left behind by Marlowe months before. His protests ignored, he was dragged off – ominously – to Bridewell where he was first questioned as to what his attitude was to blasphemy. Kyd, at a loss to understand why he should be asked such a thing, assured his interrogators that he loathed it and, no, he had never said anything that could be construed to the contrary. It worsened. When the interrogation then turned to treason he became really frightened, unable to understand what his questioners were hinting at since he had never involved himself in political matters. He was even more at a loss as to why they were so interested in Marlowe and what it was he was supposed to have done. If they were so concerned then why did they not ask him themselves? At the end of the interrogation, utterly bewildered, he simply did not know how to answer them or what it really was they wanted to know. It was then that the real nightmare began as the officers, using the powers given to them under the special Order, took him down below and put him to the rack to extract the information they required. This they achieved, Kyd offering to put his name to anything they wanted if it would stop the pain.

Six days later, on 18 May, a warrant was issued for Marlowe's arrest at Scadbury: 'Warrant to Henry Maunder one of the Messengers of Her Majesty's Chamber to repair to the house of Thomas Walsingham in Kent, or to any other place where he shall understand Christopher Marlowe to be remaining, and by virtue hereof to apprehend and bring him to the Court in his Company. And in case of need to require aid.' By this time poor Kyd had signed (as well as he could after having his limbs dislocated), the first of the two statements he was forced to make. It is a pathetic document in which he rakes together everything he had ever heard Marlowe say, drunk or sober, when ranting on of an evening in the tavern or holding forth backstage at the theatre. Marlowe had made jokes about the divine scriptures, mocked prayers, had argued against the holy writings of many of the prophets and other such men. He had said that St Paul was little better than a juggler, that the prodigal son's portion was but four nobles which did not seem very much of an inheritance, that things deemed to have been done by Divine Power could just as well have been done by men and probably were. Most damning, and all too likely given Marlowe's love of the outrageous, he was also alleged to have said that 'John was Jesus' Alexis. I cover it with reverence and trembling,' adds Kyd, 'that is that Christ did love him with an extraordinary love.'[5]

The story of Marlowe's last ten days of life is lit with a lurid glow. He was duly arrested and brought to London to appear before the Star Chamber, a fate feared by all. Which is when it all becomes distinctly odd. Not for Marlowe the rack in the bowels of Bridewell although the allegations made against him included both blasphemy and treason. 'This day Christopher Marlowe of London, gentleman, being sent for by warrant from their Lordships, has entered his appearance accordingly for his Indemnity herein, and is commanded to give his daily attendance to their Lordships until he shall be licensed to the contrary.' He was then released, in spite of the gravity of the charges, on his promise to return and sign in every morning. Ten days later he was dead in Deptford, 'stab't with a dagger' through the eye, the received wisdom for several centuries being that it had come about following a quarrel in a tavern kept by a Mistress Eleanor Bull over who should pay the reckoning which, given his previous record, would not have caused any surprise.

That doubt was finally cast on the official version is due almost entirely to a brilliant piece of detective work carried out in 1925 by the American scholar, J.L. Hotson.[6] Following the inquest on his death, Marlowe was hastily buried in the churchyard of St Nicholas, Deptford, the name of his killer wrongly transcribed as 'ffrancis archer'. Hotson, fascinated by the subject, was told of a tradition that Marlowe had in fact been killed by a man called 'Ingram' and so he began searching through documents of the period in the Public Record Office until he came across a reference to an Ingram Frizer in a deed relating to a property transfer. But when he turned his attention to more important documents, neither the inquisitions of post mortems nor the Assize Rolls yielded anything. Then it occurred to him to look under pardons for the relevant date and there he found a brief entry 'granted to Ingram Frizer (sc. for homicide) in self-defence'. If this was what he was looking for then there had to be a cross-reference to an indictment or inquest but by then it was the end of the afternoon and the office was about to close. Fired with a desire to know if he was right and after a sleepless night, Hotson was outside the door when it opened the next morning, ready to follow every clue 'until by examining every item listed under Kent, I found at length what I wanted. The Writ and Inquisition were preserved and legible.'

The document (in Latin) lists the names of the jury members called to Deptford on 1 June 1593 'upon the view of Christopher Morley [*sic*] there lying dead and slain'. There follows the version of events as given to the coroner: that Marlowe, accompanied by three men, Frizer, Nicholas Skeres and none other than Robert Poley, he of Babington Plot fame, had met in the room of a widow, Eleanor Bull, passed time together and later walked in the garden, then returned to the room for supper, during or after which Marlowe, without warning and following some angry words, had attacked Frizer, which could have happened – except that the description of the event simply does not make sense.

Frizer, we are expected to believe, was sitting on a bench between Skeres and Poley eating his supper when Marlowe suddenly wrenched Frizer's own dagger 'from his belt and cut him on the head'. The three men were sitting so close together on the bench that Frizer could not properly defend himself but, without moving from his seat, he somehow managed to grasp Marlowe's dagger hand and, in pushing hand and arm away, inadvertently drove the dagger into Marlowe's eye socket '. . . and so it befell in the affray that the said Ingram, in defence of his life, with the dagger aforesaid to the value of 12*d* [pence] gave the said Christopher then and there a mortal wound over his right eye to the depth of two inches and the width of one inch; of which mortal wound the aforesaid Christopher Morley then and there instantly died.' The document is signed not by the ordinary Deptford coroner but by the Queen's coroner, Sir William Danby. Whether the jurors believed that a man who had the freedom to move about could have been so stabbed by a man sitting on a bench in front of him trapped between two others, or had it made known to them that they had better appear to do so, they duly cleared Frizer of murder on the grounds of self-defence.

Immediately after his death a number of rumours circulated: that he was struck down by God for blaspheming in the street, that he had died in a quarrel over a lewd wench (somewhat unlikely), that he was killed in a street brawl, but soon the tale of the row over the reckoning became the accepted version. Until Hotson's discovery the true identity of Marlowe's killer was not known, nor were those of the other two members of the party present when apparently Marlowe and Frizer fought for their lives. But Poley, as we know, was a highly experienced agent in the secret service and Skeres, it turns out, a part-time agent who had worked with him in infiltrating the Babington Plot, while Ingram Frizer actually lived on the Scadbury estate and was used by Thomas Walsingham for work such as debt-collecting. Frizer had recently been involved in a court case in which he had defrauded a young man out of a substantial sum of money using a confidence trick worthy of one of today's television rogues – a scam, by the by, for which for some unknown reason he was not punished. He had agreed to lend the young innocent a sum of money against an IOU, but when the lad arrived to collect the cash Frizer gave him only half of it and a bag of worthless old guns, telling him he could sell them to make up the rest. The lad, of course, discovered nobody wanted them and so found himself owing twice the amount he had actually been loaned by Frizer. It was at this stage that his mother stepped in and took Frizer to court.

As to the 'tavern' of legend, there is no record in Deptford of any tavern kept by a woman of the name of Eleanor Bull, although such records exist with regard to other inns and taverns in the area, and their landlords or landladies, during the same period. But it was never claimed during the inquest that the event took place in a tavern, only that Marlowe was killed in 'a room in the house of a certain, Eleanor Bull, widow'. More recent research, in the run-up to the four hundredth anniversary of Marlowe's death in 1993, revealed that there was indeed an Eleanor Bull living in Deptford and that she had friends in very high places, being related both to Blanche Parry, the Queen's Chief Gentlewoman of the Privy Chamber and Robert Cecil himself. The most logical explanation, given the work undertaken by Poley and Skeres, is that she ran what we would now describe as a 'safe house'.[7]

So, if the story of the tavern quarrel does not ring true and as we know that although Marlow, had been arrested he was out on bail, free to come and go as he pleased, why was he killed? His death still provokes far more questions than answers. Was he still working for the secret service? If not, and no one who has ever undertaken that kind of dark work ever escapes from it entirely, did he know too much and had somehow become a danger to those who were? Was it thought he might blurt out in drink details of that secret world of which he had once been part? Did he hold information that might have fingered others had he been brought to trial? There are a number of twentieth-century examples of notorious, heavy-drinking, homosexual, Cambridge-educated spies who even at that later date would have been open to blackmail. How much more vulnerable would a gay man in 1590s London be to such a threat when officially homosexuality was a capital offence, although a blind eye appears to have been taken so long as it was not too overt – at least where the nobility was concerned.

One idea put forward by Charles Nicholls in *The Reckoning* is that Marlowe, whose own hands were far from clean, was used as an unwitting agent by Essex in an attempt to destroy his rival, Ralegh.

Another reason might be Marlowe's involvement with Ralegh and the School of the Night and that Cecil, still insecure in his position as Acting Secretary to the Privy Council, saw Marlowe not only as a dangerous ex-spy but as a persuasive dramatist, exposing ignorant audiences to a whole range of new and deeply subversive ideas. Lastly, what part, if any, did Marlowe's long-term patron and possible lover, Thomas Walsingham, play in the affair, since he was finally about to be married and regularly employed Frizer? One supposition is that while he might have had no direct hand in it, he felt it convenient to turn a blind eye to what had happened, taking Frizer back into his service after he had been pardoned.

We will never know what prompted Marlowe to go all the way out to Deptford. Was he persuaded that he could be smuggled out of the country to the continent and so avoid standing trial and that he might well be able to return once things had cooled down? If so, what better person to suggest it than his old secret service colleague, Robert Poley, who regularly travelled as a courier between Deptford and Holland. If this was the case then Marlowe, shrewd as he was, might well have considered the possibility that he was walking into a trap but took the risk anyway since he had nothing to lose when a trial on either one of such serious charges could only lead to his death. Whatever the truth, Marlowe's murder remains one of history's most fascinating mysteries.

Meanwhile Kyd, unaware that Marlowe was dead, still languished in Bridewell. He made a second statement which adds little to the first except that in it he alleges Marlowe had once told him it was all one to him whether he served Elizabeth of England or James of Scotland, which leaves one wondering if he had undertaken a mission or missions to Edinburgh on behalf of the Crown. Certainly Robert Poley did. Again Kyd swears that he neither condoned blasphemy nor spoke treason. The authorities did not, however, have to rely entirely on Kyd for there is also the infamous 'Note' of the informer Richard Baines, who had been employed specifically to monitor Marlowe's activities. It is a lengthy document which repeats information already given by Kyd along with additional material including 'that one Ric Cholmley has confessed he was persuaded by Marlowe to become an Atheist' (Cholmley was a spy who had been placed in Ralegh's circle); that 'the Indians and many authors of antiquity have assuredly written about 16,000 years ago', whereas Adam 'is proved to have lived within 6,000 years'; and, notoriously, 'all that love not tobacco and boys are fools'.[8]

On 28 June 1593 Frizer received his official pardon from the Queen, was released from prison and returned to Scadbury. Within a comparatively short time he was given a gift of lands and rents belonging to the Duchy of Lancaster and, in 1611, was made one of two certified assessors for Eltham and, something of a joke given his past history, an officer of various charities, being described as 'one of sixteen good and lawful men of the county'.

A warrant for payment, made out to Poley and signed by the Vice Chamberlain at the Court on 9 June 1593 is for 'carrying of letters on her Majesty's special and secret affairs of great importance from the Court at Croydon on 8 May 1593 to the Low Countries to the town of The Hague in Holland and for returning back with letters of answer to the Court at Nonsuch on 8 June 1593 *being in her Majesty's service all throughout the aforesaid time* (my italics). But, as we know, Poley was already back in England on 30 May and at Eleanor Bull's house in Deptford. Poley continued in the secret service until into the next century.

In March 1595 Nicholas Skeres was arrested at the house of a man called Williamson, who had testified against Robert Poley. He was imprisoned first in the Counter Prison to await further examination, then transferred to Newgate, and finally to Bridewell after which 'he was never seen again. . .'. A man called Richard Baines, who may have been the informer, was hanged at Tyburn on 6 December 1594.

The last words on the previous twelve months and their aftermath must go to Thomas Nashe, so closely associated with Greene, Watson and Marlowe. He wrote his cycle of verses, *Summer's Last Will and Testament*, at the end of 1593, although it was not published until eight years later. It is officially dedicated to the victims of 'King Pest' who had ruled so savagely for so long, but he must also have had in mind the friends who had died so recently:

> Haste therefore each degree
> To welcome destiny,
> Heaven is our heritage
> Earth but a player's stage.
> Mount we unto the sky.
> I am sick, I must die.
> Lord have mercy upon us

The deaths drew a line under the first creative surge of theatrical endeavour. With Greene, Marlowe and then Kyd now gone, alone in the spotlight, centre-stage, stands the single towering talent which was to dominate the English theatre then and for centuries to come: William Shakespeare.

SEVEN

Deaths and Entrances

> . . . what things we have seen
> Done at the Mermaid! Heard words that have been
> So nimble and so full of subtle flame,
> As if that every one from whence they came
> Had meant to put his whole wit in a jest,
> And had resolved to live a fool the rest of his dull life.
>
> Francis Beaumont to Ben Jonson

In the December of 1593 Thomas Kyd, broken in mind and body, finally limped out of Bridewell having unknowingly been forced to betray his colleague even after that colleague's death. When finally told that Marlowe was dead he wrote that he did not like slandering the dead, 'thus much have I dared in the greatest cause which is to clear myself of being thought an Atheist which some swear he was'. Never charged with any offence and having suffered mightily, he now found himself alone in a cold world, spurned and ignored by his fellow dramatists. Within months he was dead.

We do not know what impact the arrests of Marlowe and Kyd and the subsequent deaths of both had on the rest of the theatrical world, but there are hints. Ben Jonson, in a poem entitled 'On Inviting a Friend to Supper', warns against ever including 'Poley' among the guests, while Shakespeare's reference to the 'dead shepherd' in *As You Like It*, not to mention the line he gives to Touchstone in the same play, 'it strikes a man more dead than a great reckoning in a little room', suggests that it is likely to have been considerable.

But life goes on and was gradually returning to normal. In 1594 the Lord Chamberlain, Lord Hunsdon (who was either the Queen's nephew or her half-brother depending on which theory you believe), formally became patron to Burbage's company. The first theatre to open full-time after the plague was finally over was one at Newington Butts on the outskirts of Southwark, about which we know almost nothing except that for a period it was shared by both the Lord Admiral's and the Lord Chamberlain's Men. By the summer of 1594 the theatre companies were clamouring for the reopening of all the theatres, especially the Rose, the prolonged closure of which had severely affected not only the finances of Henslowe and the Companies of the Lord Admiral's and Lord Strange's Men, but also the takings of the hundreds of watermen who had become reliant on ferrying theatregoers over the Thames to the Bankside.

In June the Privy Council received a number of petitions on the subject. The first was on behalf of Lord Strange's Men who complained that they were finding it increasingly intolerable and a great charge to be forever travelling around the country trying to scrape a living and that if they did not soon have a London base in which to play they would be unable to entertain the Queen when next she commanded them to do so. The Rose, they wrote, was essential not only to them 'but by reason of the passage to and from the same by water, is a great relief to the poor watermen there. And our dismission [*sic*] thence in this long vacation, is to those poor men a great hindrance'.

Another petition (which is in poor condition) was delivered by the watermen themselves who 'in the most humble manner complain and sue unto your good lordships, your poor supplicants and, daily, the orators [of] Phillipp Henslo [*sic*] . . . had much help and relief for us, our poor wives and children, by means of the resort of such people to the said Playhouse'. Therefore would they please, please allow the reopening of the Rose for the sake of all concerned. The various petitions finally bore fruit and the Privy Council conceding that the theatre at Newington Butts was not altogether a suitable venue, admitted that the public was finding life tedious without access to plays, and accepted that the poor watermen needed to be relieved. This therefore being the case, 'the Rose may be at liberty, without any restraint, so long as it shall be free from infection or sickness'.[1]

So the theatres reopened. It was not, however, entirely the end of the Marlowe affair for Robert Cecil finally decided to move against the School of the Night, setting up an official inquiry at Cerne Abbas in Dorset (close to Ralegh's country home, Sherborne Castle), under the auspices of the High Commission in Causes Ecclesiasticus: its brief to investigate various 'blasphemous and atheistic matters'. The charges against those taking part in Ralegh's discussions have a familiar ring to anyone acquainted with either the allegations in Kyd's confession or the Baines's Note, but all the investigators could come up with after deliberating for weeks was that one of those attending was said to have dried tobacco on leaves torn from his Bible, that Ralegh had doubts as to the immortality of the soul, plus a few other pieces of hearsay in a similar vein. Among those questioned were Ralegh himself, his half-brother Sir George Carew, Thomas Allen, Thomas Walsingham, Hariot and, somewhat surprisingly, Ferdinand, Lord Strange, Earl of Derby, as, unlike the Earl of Northumberland, 'Wizard Earl', he had not figured earlier.[2]

But during the investigation Lord Strange died. There were contemporary rumours to the effect that he had been poisoned because he was a Catholic, though this seems unlikely given that his loyalty to Queen Elizabeth had never been in doubt.

Modern medicine suggests a more likely cause: dysentery followed by kidney failure. Sixteenth-century poisoners are given far more credit than is their due. Sheer lack of hygiene in food preparation, not to mention the absence of refrigeration, were sufficient to do the job for them. The inquiry dragged on for a while and a number of depositions were taken on oath, but no one was ever brought before either the Star Chamber or the Privy Council, nor was any action taken against Ralegh or any other member of his circle. In the end nothing came of the enquiry and the Commission simply gave up.

During the three years following Marlowe's death Shakespeare was writing prolifically. He had now become one of the sharers in the company of the Lord Chamberlain's Men, the others being Richard Burbage, Will Kempe (before he left for Norwich), Thomas Pope,

John Hemings, William Sly, Henry Condell, George Bryan and Augustine Phillips. For those who still seek to prove that Sir Francis Bacon, Marlowe (who had somehow survived Deptford) and even Queen Elizabeth (in between running the country) wrote Shakespeare's plays, one has to ask how on earth the actors and sharers in the Lord Chamberlain's Company, let alone the Burbages, could have been so fooled. He was indeed the house dramatist, but *any* playwright of the day would have been expected to be on hand to make any alterations and rewrites that might be needed, just as they are today. That Shakespeare's was, and is, a towering talent is without dispute but there is little doubt that so prestigious a patron helped to establish his place at the top of the hierarchy of dramatists who, over the next ten years, started writing for the theatre.

The new talent differed in a number of ways from the old University Wits or their colleagues, even though their backgrounds were not dissimilar and it appears that they felt no necessity to give themselves a title which identified them. By the mid-1590s playgoing in purpose-built buildings was no longer a novelty but an accepted part of London entertainment; audiences were becoming increasingly sophisticated and expected a whole range of different kinds of drama sumptuously costumed and preferably with exciting stage effects. Nor, with the possible exception of Ben Jonson, did the new breed of dramatists consider themselves to be rarefied beings but, rather, hardworking professionals, hired to provide scripts to order. In this climate Henslowe's system proved particularly effective, offering, as has already been pointed out, an advance upfront for one or more writers who would then, if the play was delivered on time and accepted by the actors, be ensured a production at the end of it. Whatever we may feel now about the quality of the writing, whether that of Shakespeare, Jonson, Middleton or Webster with his extraordinary imagery, there was no long gestation or writing period, no time for agonising over every act or scene, let alone every line. The texts were certainly not written with the idea that centuries later they would be pored over by scholars looking for nuances in every phrase. Anyone who has ever worked on a new play today is well aware of how a script has to be altered, often due to practicalities such as costume changes, how many actors are available, and other such mundane essentials. Whole theses have been written around why a character in classical drama leaves the scene when he does when the real reason might well be that the actor in question had to play at least two parts and exited at that point so that he could change his costume, add a beard, and appear a scene later as somebody else.

The demand for new material was now insatiable. As Sir Trevor Nunn once put it, it must have been rather like Hollywood in the 1930s, sucking in talent from all over the place, throwing writers together to work on a script whether they were compatible or not. One reason was because it was almost unknown for a play to be given two consecutive performances; the programme would change daily and the actors and sharers would see to it that one play was up and running while another was in rehearsal and yet another half finished, the hard-pressed hack scribbling away late into the night. Meanwhile, laboriously and possibly with the help of a hired scrivener, the bookman had to ensure that each part was written out on a separate sheet or roll, from which the word 'role' comes, to hand to actors each time a new play went into production. There would be only a handful of copies of the entire script (one to be lodged at Stationer's Hall), possibly only two, and the actors had to keep their wits about them as only their cue lines appeared on their rolls. This must often have led to some confusion and explains Quince's testy note to the actor playing Thisbe in *A Midsummer Night's Dream*: 'you must not speak that yet; that is your answer to Pyramus: you speak all your part at once, cues and all'. One reason for registering the play at Stationer's Hall was to try and ensure the script was not pirated by a rival company and the bookman was held responsible for keeping the scripts safe.

Possibly because of their workload, the lifestyles of many of the new writers were not as consciously flamboyant or outrageous as those of Greene or Marlowe, although that is not to say that they did not get drunk, fight, or end up before the local Justice of the Peace to be fined or put in prison for disorderly conduct, debt, manslaughter or, if more rarely, because the content of a play had caused offence to someone important or in authority or both. Ben Jonson was to end up imprisoned for both this last and manslaughter.

The new work began appearing in the mid-1590s, dramatists coming as it were on stream from then until the early 1600s. By the mid-1590s to 1600 there were also two new theatres on the Bankside demanding new material. The first was the Swan, built in 1596 by Francis Langley, and it is the famous sketches of its interior by Johannes de Witt that have given us a good idea of what the other playhouses of the amphitheatre type looked like inside. But both the Rose and the Swan were to have a far more important rival. No doubt the Burbages had noted the growing popularity of the Bankside as a theatrical venue in general, and the success of the Rose in particular, and might well have considered building another theatre across the river anyway but as it happened they were overtaken by events.

The land on which The Theatre was originally built in 1586 was leased from a Giles Allen and by 1595 the lease had come up for renewal. But three years later the matter still had not been resolved for Allen and the Burbages (James and his two sons, Richard and Cuthbert) had been wrangling ever since over the terms, conditions and cost of the new lease. Allen, convinced that the Burbage family had made a fortune out of The Theatre, was demanding a vastly increased price for a new agreement and therefore refused to meet the Burbages even halfway. The Burbages, on the other hand, argued that this was not the case since in order to build The Theatre in the first place, James had borrowed the enormous sum of one thousand marks (about £660) from his father-in-law and the repayments, plus interest, had been a continual drain ever since. The position had now reached stalemate. Allen then laid it on the line: either James Burbage agreed to the new terms or he could go elsewhere, making the threat on the assumption that Burbage would realise there was nothing to be gained and would give in to his ultimatum.

He did not know his man. Taking advantage of a clause he had had inserted into the original lease which stated that if he spent more than £200 on the building he was free to dismantle it and remove it 'overnight', towards the end of 1599 James did just that.

The Theatre was taken down and its materials shipped over to the Bankside and rebuilt, much to Henslowe's chagrin, a stone's throw from the Rose. The litigation with Allen was to rumble on for several years but the winner was undoubtedly the Burbage family who now owned the biggest and best theatre of its type of its day. It was called the Globe. Whether out of pique or fear that the Globe might seriously affect his takings, Henslowe promptly built another theatre, the Fortune, north of the river in Golden Lane, Cripplegate. By the end of the decade, therefore, there were three working theatres south of the Thames, the Rose, Swan and Globe and three to the north, the old Curtain, the Fortune and another amphitheatre, the Red Bull, a playhouse with a reputation for having rather more downmarket audiences and rougher tastes than the other five.

The newcomers were ten or more years younger than their predecessors and although a decade might make little difference to a farm labourer in Warwickshire or a shopkeeper in Devon, London was a different world and, after Elizabeth's reign of over forty years, times were changing. Again with the exception of Ben Jonson, we know little in any detail of the lives of the dramatists and some remain very shadowy figures. It was the work that mattered, not the writer nor practitioner and the playwrights, however popular, had little or no status in the latter years of Elizabeth or the early reign of King James I. Only a few had the right even to describe themselves as 'gentlemen', and they leave behind no chroniclers.

We know from the *Thomas More* script that Thomas Dekker, pamphleteer, essayist and reporter, was already involved in the theatre scene in the early 1590s, as was Thomas Heywood, although neither had as yet made their individual mark. Heywood, born in Lincolnshire and the son of a clergyman, was first an actor, then a prolific writer of plays and pageants, claiming at one time that he had written some two hundred which seems unlikely. Few scripts survive, however, the two best known being *Fair Maid of the West* and *A Woman Killed with Kindness*.

John Webster, who was, according to T.S. Eliot, so 'much possessed by death, And saw the skull beneath the skin', was the son of a wealthy coachmaker. The family lived in Hosier Lane, near Smithfield, and possibly that 'possession' or obsession with death had something to do with the fact that he was born within earshot of the bell that rang before the executions of Newgate prisoners and in a parish in which the vicar, John Rogers, the very first of Queen Mary's martyrs, had been burned at the stake in front of his wife and children on 4 February 1555. The first mention of his working in the theatre is when he was advanced money by Henslowe to write a play with Dekker, Thomas Middleton and the poet Michael Drayton called *Caesar's Fall,* and another on what for him would seem a most unlikely subject: *Christmas Comes But Once a Year.* The two great plays for which he is known, *The Duchess of Malfi* and *The White Devil,* both based on true historical incidents, show the blackest of creative imaginations.

If Francis Beaumont is to be believed, one of the playwright's favourite drinking places was the Mermaid Tavern on the north bank of the Thames, close to Blackfriars. Beaumont was the younger half of Beaumont and Fletcher, the two writers almost always being referred to as if they were indivisible, a kind of Elizabethan/Jacobean Gilbert and Sullivan partnership. Both were the sons of gentlemen. Beaumont, the youngest son of Sir Francis Beaumont, Justice of the Common Pleas, went up to Pembroke College, Oxford, but left after a year and was entered as a member of the Inner Temple, having been expected to follow his father into the law. He was, however, able to indulge his liking for the theatre as, unlike the rest of his contemporaries, he had no money worries, having been left part of a substantial estate. John Fletcher had no such financial security. When he was born his father was the Vicar of Rye but soon rose rapidly up the ecclesiastical ladder, first becoming Chaplain to the Queen, then holding two bishoprics in London. But he died suddenly in 1596 leaving nine surviving children and a mountain of debt. The two men started writing together almost at once and there has been much speculation as to the nature of their undoubtedly close friendship and working partnership and exactly how intimate it was. John Aubrey, ever the gossip, wrote of Beaumont 'that there was a wonderful consimility [*sic*] of fancy between him and Master John Fletcher which caused that dearness of friendship between them. . . . They lived together on the Bankside, not far from the Playhouse, both bachelors; lay together; had one Wench in the house between them which they did so admire; the same clothes and cloak between them.' Of their working relationship he wrote, 'I have heard Dr. John Earles, since Bishop of Sarum, who knew them say that Mr. Beaumont's main business was to lop the overflowings of Mr. Fletcher's luxuriant and flowing wit'.[3]

One of the very finest, and most underrated, of the second wave of dramatists is undoubtedly Thomas Middleton, born in London and the son of a comfortably-off builder, William Middleton, described as a 'citizen and tiler and bricklayer . . .'. His father died when he was five, leaving him both money and an interest in family property but by the time he was of an age to find it of use, much of it had disappeared due to his mother's unfortunate second marriage. Seven months after his father's death she married Thomas Harvey, a grocer who had lost all his own money backing a disastrous expedition led by Richard Grenville and Walter Ralegh, and who had been looking for a chance to recoup his losses ever since. Anne Middleton must have seemed easy prey for a man on the lookout for a wealthy and attractive widow and once he had married her, Harvey did everything he could to get his hands on her and her children's bequests, a theme of which Middleton was later to make a great deal of use. The situation continued amid growing acrimony until, in spite of the threat of litigation, Anne threw him out of her home. Middleton did go up to Queen's College, Oxford, but there is no record of his taking a degree there and he soon became known for 'daily accompanying the players'. It does appear that, unlike many of his theatrical friends, he actually made a happy marriage even if he and his family were perennially hard up. His wife Mary, or Magdalen, Marbeck was the daughter of a clerk of Chancery, Edward Marbeck, a granddaughter of the composer and musician John Marbeck and niece to the Provost of Oriel, Dr Roger Marbeck, and it is thought likely therefore that she had been well educated. It is possible that the couple first met through her brother Thomas who was an actor. Middleton most certainly provides some of the very finest roles for women, possibly because he was influenced from his early years by a strong-minded mother and elder sister and also by his wife. Good or bad, Middleton's women are real women.

Later toilers on the theatre scene include John Ford, John Marston and Cyril Tourneur, the latter the most obscure of all of them, but they were soon to be overshadowed by Ben Jonson. Jonson, a posthumous child, was born in 1572 a month after the death of his father, a figure shrouded in mystery the antiquity and nobility of whose ancestry was to grow over the years with the telling. His mother promptly married a bricklayer who, unlike Middleton's father, was not comfortably off, and a trade of which Jonson was reminded every time he fell out with Henslowe who was wont to refer to him disparagingly as 'the bricklayer's son' or merely as 'the bricklayer'. He grew up in Westminster and became a scholar at Westminster School, one of the best in London, and remained proud of the education he had received there, particularly his knowledge of classical languages which enabled him to disparage Shakespeare for having only 'small Latin and less Greek'. But it seems he was not encouraged to go on to university and on leaving school was apprenticed to his stepfather with a view to becoming a master bricklayer.

However, he soon tired of laying bricks and ran off to the wars in the Low Countries where, he was to brag later, he did great things including challenging a crack swordsman to face-to-face combat in front of the opposing armies, killing him and taking his armour. Jonson was nothing if not an excellent teller of tales. Sometime in 1592 or 1593 he returned to England penniless and jobless and married an Anne Lewis, of whom we know even less than we do of Anne Hathaway. At best they rubbed along. Jonson described her as a 'a shrew but honest' and they had several children, two of whom died in infancy, events which he recorded in moving verse.

Shortly after his marriage, he decided to become an actor. Possibly it was because he was not accepted by any of the London companies that, in order to learn the trade, he spent his brief acting career out on the road with a company of strolling players, a fact of which Dekker was to remind him during what later became known as 'the

Poets' War'. It seems, wrote Dekker 'that thou has forgot how thou amblest (in leather pilch) by a play wagon in the highway, and took mad Ieronimo's part to get service among the Mimics', which presumably means that at some stage he played the leading role in Kyd's *Spanish Tragedy*. He finally returned to London, however, and by 1597 he had attached himself to Henslowe's company and the Rose Theatre. The attachment was to be sporadic. Jonson would spend the rest of his theatrical life going from one theatre company to the next having rows, which would then be followed either by reconciliations (often brief) or sulking in fits of pique. Jonson was a big man in every way, in size and personality, an evening in his company once described as being like listening to a big drum being beaten in a small room.

According to Henslowe, on 28 July 1597 he advanced Jonson £4 'to be repaid on demand' and on 2 December of the same year, he notes in his *Diary*, 'lent unto Bengamin Jonson upon a booke which he was to write for us before Crysmas next after the date hereof which he showed the plot unto the companie, I have lent him in readie money the sum of . . .'; the amount is left blank. On yet another occasion he paid Jonson one pound for a play which Jonson never delivered. Initially Jonson appears to have collaborated with other dramatists on plays which are now lost. One of these was *Page of Plymouth* which he wrote with Dekker and which was, like *Arden of Faversham*, based on a real murder for which a Ulalia Page and her lover, George Strangwidge, were hanged in Barnstable in 1589. Another lost play is *The Isle of Dogs* which he wrote with one of the surviving University Wits, Thomas Nashe. It is presumed to have been a satire of some kind, though there is no record of its subject matter, but whatever it was, it obviously caused deep offence, so much so that Jonson ended up in prison, Nashe having legged it back to Great Yarmouth before he could be arrested, along with one of Henslowe's actors, Gabriel Spenser. Dating is uncertain but the incident is thought to have taken place sometime between the July and December of 1597 when Henslowe lent him more money.

The next year, however, almost proved fatal for Jonson. He had collaborated on two other lost plays, *Robert II of Scotland* and

Richard Crookback (yet another attempt to cash in on the popularity of Shakespeare's *Richard III*), when he found himself in real trouble. He had finally written an original play of his own, *Every Man in His Humour* and was touting it around hoping for a production. Sources differ as to whether it had a production before or after the event which almost took him to the scaffold. The story is mentioned, briefly, by an appalled Henslowe in a letter to Alleyn who was again out on tour, this time accompanied, unusually, by his wife, Joan. Henslowe had, he wrote, 'hard and heavy news to tell. . . . Since you were with me, I have lost one of my company which hurteth me a great deal, that is Gabriel, for he is slain in Hog's Fields at the hands of Beng. Jonson, Bricklayer, therefore I would fain have a little of your counsel if I could, this with hearty commendations to you and my daughter and likewise the rest of our friends. I end from London the 26 September 1598.'[4]

This was the very same Gabriel Spenser who had shared Jonson's first sentence of imprisonment and who was an important member of the Lord Admiral's Men, being one of the sharers. One can only surmise that bad feeling had existed between the two of them ever since. He was talented but, like Jonson, had a short fuse and two years earlier he had quarrelled with a goldsmith's son in Shoreditch; when the young man had picked up a copper candlestick and threatened to throw it at him, Spenser had attacked him with his undrawn sword, scabbard and all, cracking him over the head and making a gash, according to the inquest report, six inches deep. The unfortunate young fellow had died three days later.

It is impossible to sort out who started the fight and whether it was a sudden coming to blows or, as Jonson told it, a more formal meeting in Hogsden's Fields. Jonson's version of events is that he had, fair and square, fought a duel with Spenser, not merely set on him looking for a fight, and 'had killed his adversary' even though he had been wounded in the arm and Spenser's sword 'was ten inches longer' than his (a story very similar to that about his exploits in the wars in the Low Countries). It seems the authorities were not at first convinced and Jonson was imprisoned and threatened with the death penalty. He saved himself by using the cunning ploy resorted to by the literate of the day, pleading 'benefit of clergy'. To do this one had to be able to read from the Bible what was known as 'the neck verse', the first verse of Psalm 51, which felons able to claim 'benefit of clergy' had to read out in Latin to prove their literacy and so avoid the gallows: 'Have mercy upon me, O God, according to thy loving kindness: according unto the multitude of thy tender mercies blot out my transgressions. Wash me thoroughly from mine iniquity and cleanse me from my sin.' Some people learned it off by heart just in case, especially if they were lowlife and unable to read.

The Middlesex Sessions Rolls notes that Benj. Jonson killed Gabriel Spenser on 22 September 1598 in the Fields by Shoreditch (not far from where Marlowe had taken part in the famous fight in Hog Lane), with a three shilling rapier. That he was then tried at the Old Bailey, convicted on his own confession of felonious homicide and although he had escaped the death penalty, was still taken to Tyburn and there branded on his left thumb with the 'Tyburn T'.

Whether or not he placed his play before or after his ignominious trip to Tyburn, its production directly involves Shakespeare for it was first performed in 1598 by Burbage's company and we know from the list of actors, prefixed to the play in the Folio of Jonson's work in 1616, that Shakespeare's name is written opposite the role of Mr Knowell. This does not necessarily prove this was the part he actually played, only that he took part in its first performance. Soon Jonson was to be in trouble again, but enough for the present. We will leave him for a while drinking with his friends in Mermaid Tavern.

EIGHT

A Visit to the Playhouse

A play's a true transparent crystal mirror,
To show good minds their mirth, the bad their terror.
                    Thomas Heywood, *Apology for Actors* (1607)

Theatre was now fully professional, employing substantial numbers of actors, dramatists, apprentices, stage staff, scenery, costume and wig makers. But what of the vital element without which it would all have been pointless? Enter the audience. So who were they? Playhouse audiences crossed every social and economic boundary, from the patron and his noble friends (although he could also arrange for his players to perform at one of his houses), to the 'groundling', hard-pressed to scrape a living sufficient to give him one good meal a day. Certainly there would have been the well off and those who had been to college or, at the very least, were able to read and write but the majority would have been illiterate, which is why very often a play is preceded either by a dumbshow giving a brief résumé of the plot (as in the play within the play in *Hamlet*), or an actor coming on (as described by Dekker) to present a Prologue speech explaining the nature of the piece the audience is about to see. A good example of this is the Chorus in Shakespeare's *Henry V*. What was being offered, in fact, was the equivalent of today's programme notes.

While we know that audiences were often noisy and that many of them might choose bear-baiting or a Tyburn hanging as their next choice of entertainment, what almost all of them most certainly had was an ability to listen. Their attention span was far greater than that of an average audience, indeed the average person today for obvious reasons. There was no Elizabethan equivalent of zapping around the television stations or surfing the net. They were used to taking in information through their ears, not least because from childhood they were forced to listen to long sermons of a Sunday.

As for the language of Shakespeare or the King James Bible, considered far too difficult for most of today's students, it was not even then normal everyday speech, as we know from exchanges between the women in the *Merry Wives of Windsor* or the mechanicals in *A Midsummer Night's Dream*. But the rich verse and heightened prose of Marlowe and Shakespeare and the convoluted texts of Ben Jonson were accepted and understood, along with the wordplay and punning so beloved of the Elizabethans. Most of all, people loved a good story at a time when the oral tradition remained strong and folk still told each other tales on a winter's night. As a consequence, when spectacle was added to narrative, along with fighting, tearing passions, great deeds, and strong, declamatory acting, then an audience would give a play their best attention.

A typical visit to the theatre at the end of the sixteenth century might go something like this. A single would-be playgoer, most likely a man since it was rare for women to go unaccompanied, having seen the latest bill posted for a performance at the Rose, will start making his way to the Bankside towards the end of the morning. By the time the first trumpet has sounded to advertise that the show will commence in an hour's time, a substantial number of people are purposefully making their way towards the playhouse, many having crossed over from the north side of the Thames either by ferry or walking across London Bridge. Some might have arranged to go as a party, others recognise friends among the crowd and link up with them. Carriages too are pushing their way through the crowds, a danger to life and limb, to deposit members of the nobility or wealthy merchants at the door.

Those with little money to spare will stand to see the show, but unless they are important or wealthy enough to have commandeered a box in advance, for those who want to sit down it is first come, first served; there are no reserved seats. As our man finally arrives outside the playhouse he is at once beset by sellers of pies, bread and cheese and fruit, although oranges, along with bottle ale will also be on sale inside. Finally he buys himself a pie to stop being pestered any further and, no, he tells a persistent whore, he does not intend to lose any chance he might have of a good seat by going behind the theatre with her for fourpence.

Time passes and still the crowd moves only slowly. The trumpet sounds again to mark the half hour. The delay is largely because everyone has to pay the entrance money for himself or his party to the gatherer on the door, who might sometimes have an assistant, but even if that is the case there will always be those without the right money or who will query their change. Then, of course, there are further delays as important parties are ushered through in front of him. Finally, with fifteen minutes to spare, our playgoer reaches the door. It costs a penny to stand, tuppence or thruppence for a seat in one of the galleries (with an additional penny or tuppence to hire a cushion), sixpence to sit on the stage and considerably more for a box. He has no wish to stand and pays his thruppence, rents himself a cushion from the cushion-hirer, and looks around the rapidly filling galleries to decide where he should sit.

He decides to make for the second gallery directly in front of the stage. To get to where he wants to go, he will have to fight his way through the milling crowds in the pit, possibly buying a couple of bottles of ale en route. Also, unless he is very green, he will be keeping a careful grasp of his purse as mingling with the throng are, of course, the denizens of the Elizabethan underworld, 'the common haunters . . . apt for pilfery, perjury, forgery, or any roguery, the very scum of rascality and baggage of the people, thieves, cutpurses, shifters, cozeners; briefly an unclean generation and spawn of vipers', as Robert Greene put it. Their easiest prey is the groundlings who can have their purses cut or pockets picked while standing absorbed in what is happening on stage. Actors dread it when a victim realises what has happened and tries to pursue a robber through the crowd yelling 'stop thief!'

Finally our man reaches the foot of the steps and looks up at the second gallery. Most of the front rows of benches are already full which is not good news. Given that a considerable amount of body heat is lost through the head, almost without exception, everyone will be wearing a hat. And what hats! Stubbes describes the hats of those attending a play in graphic detail. 'Sometimes they use them sharp on the crown, perking up like the sphere or shaft of a steeple, standing a quarter of a yard about the crown of their heads. Othersome be flat, and broad in the crown like the battlements of a house . . . and another sort are content with no kind of Hat without great bunches of feathers of diverse and sundry colours.'[1] Politely requesting the person in front of you to remove their headgear was at best likely to be met either with a straight 'no' or a blunt response to the effect that if he dislikes his seat then he knows what he can do about it. As Andrew Gurr points out in *Playgoing in Shakespeare's London* it would be an unusually modest, considerate – or warm-blooded – playgoer in any of the playhouses, indoors or out, who would remove his or her headgear during a performance.

Our man finally finds himself a space on the bench behind the front row after persuading those already occupying it to move up a bit. There was little more than eighteen inches allowed for each person on the gallery seats and a playgoer was likely to be uncomfortably squashed, not least because the average woman's dress of the day was exceedingly bulky. It is unlikely that even the wealthiest lady would attend a theatrical performance in the huge farthingales which were the height of fashion at Court, but most women would be wearing a substantial number of petticoats, have their hips padded out with buckram and, since they were eager both to see and be seen, be wearing one of their best gowns overall with a wide ruff or high collar which would add to their bulk and further impede the view of those behind; not to mention having also draped their cloaks around them; the playhouse is, after all, open to the elements even though they are under cover. As Samuel Rowlands put it in l600:

> A Buske, a Mask, a Fanne, a monstrous Ruffe,
> A Boulster for their Buttockes and such stuffe.

Finally, our man settles uncomfortably on the end of a bench where he will just about be able to see what is going on. He will

109

have to make the best of it and hopes it will not be as bad as all that for he is likely to be in the theatre for anything up to three hours or more. From the information available in the new Globe Theatre, it is suggested that there was no interval, the play being played through straight which led to a certain amount of coming and going during a performance. One reason was that public toilets in any way we might understand them did not exist, yet many of those attending the show will have drunk several pints of ale or cups of wine beforehand and so might well need to relieve themselves. Buckets were provided for this, reasonably easy for gentlemen to urinate in but how women managed is anybody's guess.

As he waits, he looks around. Some repainting has been done since his last visit, the 'heavens', the canopy over the stage, is a brilliant blue on which are painted a glittering golden sun and silver moon and stars, and the pillars holding it up boast new gilt paint. It is all very grand. Finally, the last trumpet sounds and the play begins with a spoken prologue. Audiences rather liked an actor welcoming them into the playhouse and thanking them for coming to see the play. It made them realise that his words were addressed to all those present, rich and poor alike, that each was an individual spectator of equal importance to the actors. For the same reason they also enjoyed an epilogue, especially when it was given by a player in the role of a king or duke pleading with them to show by their applause how the play had been received. It was also what turned this particular kind of entertainment into something more than an alternative to an afternoon at the bear-baiting or cockfight. It was what made it a performance.

So, for now, we will leave our man sitting on his cushion cheek-by-jowl with his neighbour, clutching his pie and his bottle ale and hoping he will not have to make use of the buckets until the end of the show.

We know that as well as being enthralled by the story and the acting, audiences expected the productions to look good, as is evident from the inventories of costumes listed in Henslowe's *Diaries*, and that many were extremely fine, made from quality materials, not cheap imitations, and that they cost a good deal. There are accounts for the buying of fine cambric for smocks and shirts, velvet and lace for caps and hats and dozens of pairs of silk long hose and silk stockings. Scores of costumes are inventoried. Among the outerwear are cloaks of 'fine green velvet', 'turquoise taffeta', 'black silk' and 'a fine . . . velvet cape bound with bugle lace and tufted lace', 'a white short cloak of satin laid with lace and lined with velvet'. There are lists of fine gowns for the women characters: 'a purple gown of silk laid with lace'; 'a yellow branched-damask petticoat with an overgown of golden taffeta with rich lace'; a 'fine morning gown for a woman and round kirtle of "buffen", pinked with "gardes" of satin'; 'a gown of silk and branched velvet embroidered in gold thread' are but a few examples.

But it was the men who were truly magnificent. Productions were, of course, played in what was then 'modern dress', although Caesar might well have worn a toga over his doublet and breeches to suggest ancient Rome or Macbeth a plaid, but the lovers who are lost in a wood near Athens in *A Midsummer Night's Dream* would be dressed in the fashion of well-off young people of the time. As for actors playing kings or nobility, they were fully expected to look the part and certainly did. Among the many male costumes listed are 'an orange tawny doublet, laid thick with gold lace', 'one blue taffeta suit', 'a pair of silver hose with satin panels', 'Tamburlaine's coat with copper lace', 'a peach satin doublet', 'a black satin doublet layered thick with black and gold lace', 'a carnation satin doublet layered with gold lace' and 'a flame-coloured doublet, pinked'. An inventory for 1598 lists a 'black velvet jerkin laid thick with black silk lace and "caneyanes" of cloth of silver' and 'a pair of hose of cloth of gold layered thick with black silk lace'.

Sometimes it is possible to follow the progress of a production through *Diary* entries. Sometime in November 1598 Henslowe notes that he bought the 'book' of a play called *The Two Angry Women of Abingdon*, presumably a potboiler, written by someone called Harry Porter. Here we run into the problems caused by those still using the old dating system when the New Year began in March, for following this we learn in 'January 1598', which in modern dating would be

January 1599, that Henslowe paid out money for costumes for the piece including a sum 'to buy taffeta for women's gowns for the *Two Angry Women of Abingdon*'. In February, Henslowe paid Porter the rest of the money for the 'book' of the play and on the twelfth of the month provided more cash for various props 'and things needed' for the production. We must assume that the show was finally put on since there is nothing to suggest it was not and it must have been well received for a little while later 'the company' persuaded Henslowe to part with money for what presumably was a sequel entitled *The Merry Women of Abingdon*.

As already noted, basic stage scenery and props also played a major part in the productions. It has been suggested that there might well have been some crude method of 'flying in' scenery using the tower, but there do not seem to be any accounts of it. Some of the bigger pieces needed would, no doubt, have been set up in advance, while stage furniture would be brought in and taken off as needed. Again we have some idea of what was in regular use from the *Diary* inventories. It includes, as well as the Hell Mouth and the cauldron for the Jew, 'Old Mahommet's Head, one rock, one cave, one tomb of Guido, one tomb of Dido, one bedstead, eight lances and one pair of stairs for Phaeton, a chime of bells and a beacon, one globe, a sceptre, a golden fleece, a bay tree, a tree of golden apples, a head of Cerberus and eight other heads, Mercury's wings and dragons' and 'one chain of dragons', green hats for Robin Hood, green coats for Robin Hood and a hobby horse, imperial crowns and ghost crowns, and something simply described as 'the City of Rome'. Some of the jewellery seems to have been real for there are several items listed as 'gold rings'. There was also expenditure on rapiers, daggers and the 'hangars' on which swords were suspended. There are also payments for musical instruments; whether for the use of company members or by musicians hired in for the occasion is not stated, but we know that music often played a part in the productions of the day. The audience, in fact, had good value for its money.

So who, as well as our man, is in the audience? For women who can persuade their husbands to let them go to the theatre it is a splendid day out, 'persuade' being the operative word since playhouses are notorious as places of assignation and very often a husband or father will prefer to accompany his wife or daughter to make sure she behaves herself. But it is very unlikely that a woman of any substance will even have thought of going to a playhouse unaccompanied; at best she would be easy game for pickpockets, at worst taken for a whore. At the very least therefore she will be accompanied by her maid, unless she is one of a party of friends who have arranged to meet up and go together. If she does have an ulterior motive for visiting the playhouse then no doubt she has made it worth her maid's while beforehand to hold her tongue. But even then she is taking a considerable risk as she can never be sure whether there is someone who knows her and her father or husband among the crowds in the theatre who will be only too eager to tell tales.

There are also other hazards. A widely circulated story is a case in point.[2] As Henry Peacham tells it:

A tradesman's wife of the Exchange, one day when her husband was following some business in the City desired him he would give her leave to go and see a play, which she had not done for seven years. He bade her take his apprentice along with her, and go; but especially to have a care of her purse which she warranted she would.

Sitting in a box, among some gallants and gallants' wenches, and returning when the play was done, she went home to her husband and told him that she had lost her purse. 'Wife,' quoth he, 'did I not give you warning of it? How much money was there in it?' Quoth she, 'Truly, four pieces, six shillings and a silver tooth-picker.' Quoth her husband, 'Where did you put it?' 'Under my petticoats, between them and my smock.' 'What!', quoth he, 'did you feel nobody's hand there?' 'Yes', quoth she, 'I felt one's hand there but did not think he had come for that. . .'

Gosson describes a scene where just such an incident could take place and be misunderstood:

You shall see such heaving and shoving, such itching and shouldering, to sit by women; such care for their garments that they be not trod on; such eyes to their laps, that no chips light in them; such pillows to their backs, that they take no hurt; such masking in their ears, I know not what; such giving them pippins to pass the time; such playing at the foot saunt without cards; such tickling, such toying, such smiling, such winking, such manning them home when the sports are ended, that it is a right comedy.[3]

As to the reaction of the audience to what they saw, there is no doubt that patriotic wars went down well, not just the obvious *Henry V* and other 'King Harry' plays, but also *Henry VI* when it dealt with the wars in France (in particular the role played by the heroic Talbot), and the anonymous play of *Edward III* that appears in collections of Shakespeare apocrypha, that is, plays which might be attributed to Shakespeare but in this instance is more likely to have been a collaborative effort. As Heywood put it: 'What English blood seeing the person of any bold English presented and doth not hug his fame and honour his valour, pursuing him in his enterprise with his best wishes and as being wrapt in contemplation, offers to him in his heart all prosperous performance, as if the performer were himself the man personated? So bewitching a thing is lively and well spirited action, that it hath power to new mould the heart of the spectator.'

Gosson, reporting the reaction of the audience to a play in which Bacchus wooed Ariadne, describes the audience as being in a transport of delight by the end of the performance. 'The beholders rose up, every man stood on tiptoe and seemed to hover over the prey, when they swore, the company swore, when they departed to bed, the company presently were set on fire, they that were married posted home to their wives; they that were single vowed, very solemnly, to be wedded.'

Glimpses of productions appear in the Simon Forman papers. He loved the theatre and, on occasion, would rush home and write an account of what he had just seen. There is an interesting insight into a performance of *Macbeth* at the Globe in which he describes the first appearance of the three witches, all too often played today as ugly women about ninety years old. In this production Macbeth and Banquo are riding through Scotland when, he reports, 'there stood before them three women fairies or nymphs. And saluted Macbeth saying three times unto him "Hail, Macbeth, king of Cawdor; for thou shalt be a king but shal beget no kings, etc." Sometimes he adds a little homily to what he had learned that afternoon. Following a play on the subject of Richard II (not Shakespeare's), he notes: 'I say it was a villain's part and a Judas kiss to hang a man for telling the truth. Beware this example of noblemen and of their fair words, and say little to them, lest they do the like by thee for thy goodwill.' He enjoyed *The Winter's Tale* (also at the Globe) and was highly amused by the rogue, Autolycus, and his trickery and how easily he cozened people into believing him. Therefore, he tells himself, one should 'beware of trusting feigned beggars or fawning fellows'. Presumably some of the performances he saw had the same effect on him as that described by Gosson, as afterwards he would race out of the playhouse either to hurl himself into the arms of 'Julia in Seething Lane', into bed with his wife, or possibly both.[4]

There was far more reaction from an Elizabethan audience then we would expect today. As with Victorian melodramas, villains were hissed and booed, heroes cheered. The groundlings in particular might well chime in with words of their own. For example when Henry V announced he was going to fight in France he was quite likely to have been greeted with the Elizabethan equivalent of 'go for it, Hal!' Even much later, Dickens wrote of a performance of *Hamlet* in which the audience took sides during the great soliloquy 'to be or not to be', some suggesting Hamlet should go ahead, kill himself and get it over with, the rest telling him to pull himself together and sort out the situation. Since the plot lines of many of the plays, most particularly those of Shakespeare, are widely known today even by those who are not regular theatregoers, we need to remember that most of the people attending an Elizabethan or early seventeenth-century production would have no idea how the story would resolve itself. Possibly Romeo and Juliet *would* marry and live happily ever after, Hamlet kill his stepfather and become King of Denmark. With regard to *Hamlet* possibly the nearest we could come to this nowadays was described by the actor Derek Jacobi who, some years ago, took part in a tour of China organised by the British Council and found it an extraordinary experience to play to audiences who did not know how it ended.

If a play was well received, then at the end of it there would be plenty of noisy applause and shouts of approval. Michael Drayton wrote of how good it was to sit in the Rose and listen to the reaction of an audience which had enjoyed the show. At the:

> Shouts and Claps at every little pause,
> When the proud Round with on every side hath rung.[5]

If it was not, then there would be no shortage of insults shouted out for all to hear or, in the worst-case scenario, various kinds of missiles thrown on stage. An extreme example of what could happen, even if his woes were self-inflicted, is recorded by John Taylor, known as 'the Water Poet'. Taylor had become so fascinated by the poets, dramatists and actors he regularly ferried across the Thames that he eventually decided he could emulate them himself. The result was reams of awful verse which he paid to have published. In 1613 he hired one of the newer theatres, the Hope, and challenged a William Fennor, who described himself as 'the King's Rhyming Poet', to a competition not only to decide who was the best poet but who could come up with the worst insults about the other's work. Fennor agreed and Taylor, after hiring the theatre, duly paid for a thousand handbills to be printed advertising the event which he then assiduously distributed throughout the City and the Bankside.

'I divulged my name in some 1000 ways and more, giving my Friends and diverse of my acquaintance notice of this Bear-garden of dainty conceits.' To ensure the appearance of Fennor, he gave him ten shillings 'in earnest of his coming to meet me'. His aim had been to attract a really big crowd and he certainly succeeded for when the big day came the theatre was packed. Taylor, in his best suit, looked out from backstage therefore on to a vast and noisy audience, the groundlings in the pit already impatient for the show to begin. He and they waited . . . and waited . . . until the awful realisation dawned on Taylor that Fennor was not going to show up and the whole audience was becoming increasingly restive. It was then that he made his big mistake. He went out on to the stage and told the audience that the contest would not be taking place and that he now proposed to read them a selection of his own works. Even had he been a better poet or a fine actor it is highly unlikely, in the circumstances, that he would have been able to hold the house. Grimly he details what happened next:

> some laughed, some swore, some stared and stamped and cursed,
> And in confused humours all out burst.
> I (as I could) did stand the desperate shock,
> And bid the brunt of many a dangerous knock.
> For now the stinkards in their ireful wrath,
> Bepelted me with loam, with stones and laths,
> One madly sits like bottle-ale and hisses,
> Another throws a stone and 'cause he misses,
> He yawns and bawls and cries Away, away . . .
> Some run to the door to get again their coin,
> And some do shift and some again purloin,
> One valiantly stept [*sic*] up upon the stage,
> And would tear down the hangings in his rage
> (God grant, he may have hanging at his end),
> That with me for the hangings did contend.
> Such clapping, hissing, swearing, stamping, smiling,
> Applauding, scorning, liking and rewriting
> Did more torment me than a Purgatory.[6]

The players at the Hope, who had turned up to see the fun, finally took matters into their own hands and offered to perform a play for the audience and, this being greeted with approval, started the show. But in spite of this Taylor refused to leave the stage and for some time attempted to continue reading his poems while the action of the play took place around him, until he finally admitted defeat and gave up.

It was partly as a way of preventing any possible trouble at the end of a play that the 'Jig' was performed although it was often noted that this made those who stayed to watch it even rowdier and also gave further opportunities to the cutpurses. Thomas Dekker notes:

I have often seen after the finishing of some worthy Tragedy or Catastrophe in the open theatres, that the scene after the epilogue hath been more black (about a nasty bawdy jig) than the most horrid scene in the play was; the stinkards speaking all things, yet no man understanding anything; a mutiny among them, yet none in danger; no tumult, yet no quietness; no mischief begotten and yet mischief borne; the swiftness of such a torrent, the more it overwhelms, breeding the more pleasure.

So, let us hope our original playgoer has enjoyed the performance whether it was of *Tamburlaine*, *Henry V* or *The Two Angry Women of Abingdon*. His problem now is to get out of the theatre through the crowds making for the door or doors; as there is no need to collect money, another gate or door might well have been opened up to let people out. Just as now, there are those who block the stairs chatting to each other, and he has to push through them. Once on the ground floor, he finds himself propelled willy-nilly towards the exits by the 'stinkards' pushing and shoving from behind, desperate to get outside and into the taverns or ordinaries. Women, aware of having spent a long time away from home, are now anxious to return to their families and force their way through as best they can. Sir John Davies, writing in 1595, described the feelings of a young man as he attempts to leave the playhouse and the real world impinges on that of the fantasy land in which he has spent the last few hours:

> For as we see it all the play house doors,
> When ended is the play, the dance and song;
> A thousand townsmen, gentlemen and whores,
> Porters and serving-men together throng,
> So thoughts of drinking, thriving, wenching, war

And borrowing money, raging in his mind,
To issue all at once so forward are,
As none at all can perfect passage find.[7]

Finally our man stumbles out into the street. His backside is sore with sitting on the edge of the bench and someone behind him has spilt bottle ale down his new doublet. But all in all it has been a good afternoon. He hears a shout from across the street and sees a friend. He goes over to him and together they go off to the Anchor tavern for a quart of ale.

NINE

Curtain Fall on the Elizabethans

> For within the hollow crown
> That rounds the temple of a king
> Keeps death his court . . .
>
> *Richard II*, III, ii

The sheer number of plays written between 1594 and 1604 is truly staggering. According to Professor Gurr, 145 plays are recorded in each of the two five-year periods 1594–99 and 1599–1604, more than at any other time in theatrical history. Looking at the various repertoires, he suggests that until the end of the century the two most famous and dominating companies, the Lord Admiral's Men and the Lord Chamberlain's Men, offered very similar repertoires, but that afterwards they developed in markedly different directions. On the grand scale Henslowe's company, based at the Rose, had always favoured epics such as *Tamburlaine*, while Burbage's preference was for histories of English kings, but having said that, both had in their repertoires plays about Henry V, Owen Tudor, Jack Straw's rebellion, King John, Richard III and Troilus and Cressida. As for comedies, one of Henslowe's most popular productions was Dekker's *The Shoemaker's Holiday* while Burbage's comedy offerings included *A Midsummer Night's Dream* and (although the dating is still a matter of contention) *Love's Labour's Lost*.

Gurr then senses a marked change in Henslowe's repertoire as his patron the Lord Admiral, Lord Howard of Effingham, becomes more powerful at Court, which might explain 'the distinctive political allegiance which can be seen in the altered repertoire of the Henslowe companies where the plays are seen to be upholding not only English Protestant values but specifically London Protestant

THE
SHOMAKERS
Holiday.
O R
The Gentle Craft.

With the humorous life of Simon
Eyre, fhoomaker, and Lord Maior
of London.

As it was acted before the Queenes moft excellent Ma-
ieftie on New-yeares day at night laft, by the right
honourable the Earle of Notingham, Lord high Ad-
mirall of England, his feruants.

Printed by Valentine Sims dwelling at the foote of Adling
hill, neere Bainards Caftle, at the figne of the White
Swanne, and are there to be fold.
1 6 0 0.

values. 'However,' he concludes, 'how much these plays were produced under a stimulus from the company's patron and how much they indicate an allegiance to a particular kind of audience and its values is not clear.'[1]

What is clear, however, is that during the late 1590s and the three years leading up to the death of the Queen in 1603 the increasingly tense and uncertain political situation in the capital impinged on all the companies as rival factions at Court jockeyed for position, the draconian persecution of Catholic dissidents continued, while overshadowing everything was the prospect of the Queen's death and the succession since she had still not officially designated James of Scotland as her heir. In such uneasy and worrying times it was particularly easy to cause unintentional offence and end up upsetting one side or another as even Shakespeare was to discover.

To catch up with what he was doing, it is necessary to backtrack a little. We know little or nothing about how often (or not) he visited his family in Stratford but in August 1596 he suffered a devastating blow with the loss of one of his twin children, his son, Hamnet. The boy was only eleven and the most likely cause of his death was some summer epidemic, possibly the plague. We do not even know whether Shakespeare reached Stratford in time to see him before he died or even if he attended the funeral. Unlike Ben Jonson on the deaths of two of his children, he wrote no moving poem on the death of his only son, although it is possible that he put his feelings into the words of the grieving mother, Constance, in *King John*.

But from then on we do know he regularly visited Stratford. By this time he was doing very well indeed and, unlike most of his fellow poets, was saving his money rather than spending it. Indeed he was so well off that in 1597 he bought himself the finest house in Stratford, New Place, and a year later he was back again, adding to what we might now describe as his property portfolio. A note to that effect dated 24 January 1598 records that 'our countryman, Master Shakespeare, is willing to disburse some money upon some . . . land or other in Shottery [his mother's home village] or near about us. He thinketh it a very fit pattern to move him to deal in the matter of four tithes. . . . If obtained, it would advance him in deed and would do us much good.' Over the years he would buy still more property, in the town in Chapel Street and out in the countryside near Rowington.[2]

He must also have known how Stratford had suffered following a fire in 1595 which destroyed over a hundred houses and cottages and left four hundred people homeless, a disaster from which Stratford had still not recovered three years later. Now, on top of everything, the townsfolk were facing increased taxation in large part to fund the wars in Ireland, and Shakespeare's old friend Richard Quiney was sent to London to petition the Queen for tax relief. But Quiney was kept hanging about in London so long waiting for some kind of a response that he finally ran out of money. With no family nearby to turn to, he wrote to Shakespeare 'craving your help with thirty shillings . . . you shall friend me much in helping me out of all the debts I owe in London'. He assures Shakespeare that he will not 'lose credit nor money by me, the Lord willing'. He had, he said, been summoned yet again to Court that very night and hoped this time to receive an answer to his petition. He concludes in haste. 'The Lord be with you and with us all amen. From the Bell in Carter Lane the 25 October 1598, yours in all kindness Richard Quiney.'[3] It seems Shakespeare obliged and the two men must have remained on good terms for Richard Quiney's son later married Shakespeare's daughter, Judith.

It was also about then that Shakespeare's brother Edmund, the youngest of the family, went to London to try his fortune as an actor, which is almost all we know of him. If he joined Burbage's company then there is no record of it, nor is he listed among those who played at the Rose. There are only two references to his ever having worked in the playhouses, both sad ones. In the Register of Burials of the church of St Saviour's, Southwark (now Southwark Cathedral) it is noted that there was 'buried 12 August 1607 Edward, son of Edmund Shakespeare, player, baseborn', and on 31 December of the same year 'Edmund Shakespeare, player, buried in the Church with a forenoon knell of the Great Bell twenty shillings'. This would be an expensive funeral for an unknown actor and was presumably paid for by his brother. The burial took place on a day so cold the Thames froze over.

So to Shakespeare's first inadvertent brush with controversy, one that was to spill over and later involve Henslowe and his stable of writers. If we accept the dates most frequently given, it was during the time when he was working hard in London while also visiting Stratford to buy property that he wrote the two parts of *Henry IV*. It might well be that visiting home ground inspired the funny, but also nostalgic, scenes set in nearby Gloucestershire; after all, the Vale of Evesham is only down the road from Stratford. The plays, with their combination of political intrigue, civil war and comedy, were instantly popular not least because they introduced to an enraptured audience one of the greatest comic characters in the English language, Sir John Falstaff. However, 'Falstaff' was not the name Shakespeare originally gave him; in the first acting scripts the fat knight was called Sir John Oldcastle. But after the first performances it soon transpired that there had been an actual Sir John Oldcastle who really had lived during the reign of Henry IV and within a very short time Shakespeare found himself in trouble, for one of that Oldcastle's descendants, Lord Cobham, was alive and well and a prominent figure at Court.

Not only that, the names of 'Oldcastle' and 'Cobham' were linked because the original Sir John had also taken the name 'Cobham' by virtue of his marriage to a Cobham heiress. To upset an influential courtier by giving the name of one of his ancestors to a lecherous rogue and liar was bad enough, but there was worse to come. It seems that the original Oldcastle's career had ended in disgrace after he had fallen out with the King and given his support to the great Welsh leader Owen Glendower (who also appears in *Henry IV Part I*), in his rising against the English. Oldcastle was further accused of aiding the Scots but when he was finally captured and brought to trial, the worst crime with which he was charged was that he had embraced the Protestant religion through the teaching of the heretic Lollards. Whether or not Shakespeare might actually have had a whiff of all this when he invented the character cannot be proved either way, but it does at least seem something of a coincidence that

Oldcastle, as well confessing his guilt for his various misdeeds, also acknowledged that he had been much given to 'pride, gluttony and lechery' and that his subsequent treasonable behaviour was due to his having lately been cast off by the King, to whom he had once been very close, much as Falstaff is by Prince Hal at the end of *Henry IV Part II.*

Oldcastle was duly hanged, then burned (hanged for treason and his body burned for heresy), but over the years the Cobham family had played down any suggestion of treason, along with his 'pride, gluttony and lechery', and reinvented and rehabilitated their relative as an early Protestant martyr. Cobham's displeasure was made clear to Shakspeare and to ensure that no further trouble or offence was given, as well as changing the name of his knight to 'Falstaff', he also inserted a note at the end of the first Quarto of *Henry IV Part II* drawing attention to the fact that this had been done 'for Oldcastle died a martyr and this is not the man'.

However, in spite of the change of name, the character seems to have remained 'Oldcastle' in the minds of those who had seen the first performances of the plays which is why, some two years later, the whole business was to erupt again. Henslowe, envious of the tremendous success of the *Henry* plays in general and Falstaff in particular, decided he too wanted a Falstaff play. But such a character could hardly be called 'Falstaff' without bringing down on him the wrath of the Lord Chamberlain's Men so, either unaware of the trouble this caused previously, or having forgotten about it, he commissioned a new play based on the adventures of the fat knight, reverting to the previous name of Oldcastle. An entry in his company's accounts for 16 October 1599 reads: 'received Thomas Downton, of Philip Henslowe, to pay Mr. Monday, Mr. Drayton, Mr. Wilson and Mr. Hathway for the first part of the *Lyfe of Sir John Ouldcasstel*, and in earnest of the second part for the use of the company, ten pounds, I say received'.[4]

We know little or nothing now of Henslowe's Oldcastle play but there is plenty of evidence of its effect. News of what was afoot immediately reawakened the wrath of the Cobham family. Lord Cobham, who had considered the matter dealt with once and for all, was furious at the very idea of yet another portrayal of his martyred relative as a roistering, bragging, ale-swigging monster. But his reaction was mild compared to that of his brother-in-law, Sir Robert Cecil, who also claimed a relationship with the original Oldcastle and was now finally confirmed in his position as Secretary to the Privy Council and one of the most powerful men in the country, if not *the* most. He was the very last person anyone would willingly want to cross. Cecil's main antagonist and enemy at Court was the young, rash Earl of Essex. It seems that Essex had first picked up the relationship between Cobham, Cecil and 'Sir John Oldcastle' when the character first appeared in Shakespeare's play and had made the most of it. Indeed in the Essex household it had become a family joke to the point that when the Earl was away from home his wife wrote to him with amusing references to that effect. Thus Henslowe's notion of cashing in on the success of Shakespeare's Falstaff came rapidly unstuck as he and his writers found that they had not only offended Cobham but were in danger of being caught up in the power struggle between Cecil and Essex. Sir John Falstaff, therefore, remained triumphant and without rivals. There was, in fact, another, anonymous Oldcastle play that attempted to put the record straight. Published in 1600, it was entitled *The True and Honourable History of the life of Sir John Oldcastle, the Good Lord Cobham. As of hath been lately acted by the Earle of Notingham his Servants.*

However the theatre world was already changing. Not only were new writers taking the place of old, there were also new actors and one of the two who had dominated the theatre scene for the last decade and more, Edward Alleyn, was now bowing out. He had been appearing on stage less and less often; it is not obvious why. Possibly he found the roles he now played no longer as rewarding as those of the heady days of Tamburlaine and Faustus, but whatever the reasoning behind it, in 1597 he sold his stock in the Lord Admiral's company (although cannily retaining his share of the theatre profits), and began buying land in Dulwich. Only Alleyn and Shakespeare in the theatrical profession of the day were that careful.

126

However Alleyn did not entirely give up what might be termed the entertainment industry. Henslowe had spent years lobbying to become the Queen's Bearmaster and when he finally achieved his ambition, Alleyn joined him as Joint Master of the Bears, a strange choice for a man who had been such a great actor. He also became a churchwarden at St Saviour's and from then on devoted his time to setting up a Foundation in Dulwich, almshouses, a chapel which was consecrated by the Archbishop of Canterbury in person, and finally the College which still exists today. It is easy to imagine that what he would have cherished beyond anything was the accolade of knighthood, something quite impossible at such a time. It would be nearly 300 years before a young man from the village of Halsetown in Cornwall, born Henry Brodribb, was to become the first theatrical knight under the name Sir Henry Irving.

But in spite of the difficult political climate, the theatre scene at the turn of the century was much enlivened by what became known as 'the Poets' War'. Its main protagonists were Ben Jonson (naturally), John Marston and Thomas Dekker. Jonson could never be described as a team player and throughout his life would be quick to give and take offence, which is what happened in 1599 when Marston presented his latest offering. In fact it was not an original piece but a rewrite of an old play called *Histriomastix* which he had resurrected. Actually he rather admired Jonson so he gave one of the leading characters, Chrisoganus, some of Jonson's best-known characteristics and habits, attributes which he was later to swear had been intended only as a compliment. That said, however, he must have realised he was taking something of a chance, given Jonson's choleric disposition. The result was as might have been expected: it is an understatement to say that Jonson took his portrayal as anything but a compliment.

Every Man In His Humour was in repertoire at the time and he immediately inserted sentences and phrases into the dialogue he had written for the character of a buffoon to suggest it was Marston. To ram the point home he had another character refer to him as 'a public, scurrilous and profane jester who could scent out a good meal three miles off'. Marston, now furious, struck back, this time with malice aforethought. His next play, *Jack Drum's Entertainment*, presented a much more obvious portrayal of Jonson in the person of 'Mr. Brabant Senior'. While the character still showed vestiges of Jonson's more likeable traits, he was also portrayed as being extremely pompous and forever pontificating on the correct way to write comedies to those who neither needed nor appreciated his advice, a trait Jonson's contemporaries found profoundly irritating.

Jonson described it as a low, insulting parody and, quick as a flash, riposted with *Cynthia's Revels*, ridiculing Marston in the role of Hedon and also, for no good reason at all, dragging in his old colleague the good-natured Thomas Dekker who had done nothing whatsoever to draw his fire. Of course the Poets' War was tremendously good for business and soon the Rose and the Globe were packed out with audiences eager to discover who was going to be insulted next. In retaliation Marston and Dekker combined their efforts in an over-the-top portrayal of Jonson as the swaggering, bombastic Lampatha Doria in *What You Will*, driving Jonson to finish his next opus, *The Poetaster*, at top speed. In this the barely disguised Marston and Dekker appear as two terrible hacks, Crispinus and Demetrius, in a Roman gallery of poetic fame in which Ovid comes first while they are rated at the very bottom of the literary scale. Points in this round were awarded to Jonson.

It is said that in the end even Shakespeare was dragged into it. It was while it was all going on that Will Kempe, who had been for so long Burbage's star comic, decided to undertake his great 'Jig' to Norwich. He was immensely popular and interpreted many of Shakespeare's early clowns but, like Tarlton before him, he found it restricting to keep to a script, and this may be what finally decided him to give up straight theatre. This can prove a dilemma even today for those who have attempted to make the transition from stand-up comic to comic actor. The theatre director Sir Peter Hall persuaded the comedian, the late Frankie Howerd, to take the role of Bottom in his film of *A Midsummer Night's Dream* but he did not enjoy being so confined within a text and refused any offers to play in Shakespeare again. However it is clear that Kempe admired Shakespeare for, apropos the Poets' War, he wrote:

Few of the university men pen plays well, they smell too much of the writer, Ovid, and that writer Metamorphosis . . . whereas here's our fellow Shakespeare puts them all down, aye, and Ben Jonson too. O that Ben Jonson is a pestilent fellow, he brought up Horace, giving our poets a pill, but our fellow Shakespeare has given him a purge that made him betray his credit.

It is suggested that the 'purge' is the character of the ludicrous Ajax in *Troilus and Cressida*. But whether Shakespeare took a hand in it or not, it seems that eventually even Jonson ran out of steam and finally grew tired of his war. In his original Preface to *The Poetaster*, spoken by Envy, he takes a number of swipes at his critics and their spy-like suggestions and 'petty whisperings'. But by the time he reaches his 'Apologetical Dialogue' at the end of the published script of the play and after describing how some with better natures had found themselves drawn into the quarrel, he declares that he is fed up with the whole business and from now on will turn his considerable talent to writing tragedy. But that was not quite the end of the matter, for Dekker, who had done nothing to offend Jonson, was still feeling sore. In his play *Satiromastix*, put on a few weeks after *Poetaster*, he actually uses one of Jonson's own characters, Captain Tucca. To make absolutely sure the audience is in no doubt who it is supposed to be, Dekker says that it would have been impossible to invent such a swaggerer. Since the play was performed by Burbage's company, presumably Shakespeare, as both a sharer and resident dramatist, was happy to go along with it. In any event for some time after this, Jonson did turn his attention to writing those tragedies now rarely, if ever, performed. But at some time he must have made it up with Marston for in 1605 both of them were to end up together in gaol.[5]

All too soon Shakespeare and the Lord Chamberlain's Men were to find themselves in a situation compared to which the offending of Lord Cobham was nothing. The origins of the position they were to find themselves in go back to 1599 when the government decided to send a major force to Ireland. There had been two further attempts

129

by Spain to land troops there, in 1596 and 1597, and by 1599 Elizabeth's intelligencers were returning with news of increased shipping movements off Corunna. Finally, after much persuasion on his part, Elizabeth agreed to her favourite, the Earl of Essex, leading the army even though his last military foray had been a failure and he had subsequently offended the Queen by his behaviour. It was not a popular move, not least with Sir Robert Cecil. Essex rode off to war in magnificent style, cheered on by the population, and the Lord Chamberlain's Men took advantage of the general feeling of patriotism to mount a performance of Shakespeare's *Henry V*. Simon Forman, who had watched and described Essex's triumphant exit from London, went home and cast the Earl's horoscope, coming up with the result that: 'There seems to be at the end of his voyage negligence, treason, hunger, sickness and death. At his return treachery shall be wrought against him; the end will be evil to himself, for he shall be imprisoned or have great trouble.' Which one has to admit would prove prophetic.

Essex's subsequent history is well known: his laid-back approach to the job of pacifying Ireland, his extravagance, the rout of his army by Hugh O'Neill at the Battle of Yellow Ford which inflicted on the English army its greatest ever defeat in Ireland, followed by his secret negotiations with O'Neill to see if he could do a deal with the Irish leader once the Queen was dead. Forman's forecast was only too accurate for his treasonable dealings were indeed betrayed to the Queen and were followed by his mad dash home, where he burst into the Queen's bedchamber to fling himself at her feet and ask for pardon. Yet again he played on her weakness for him and yet again he seemed to have got away with it and was first placed under what amounted to house arrest, then allowed his freedom so long as he did not come to Court.

It is hard not to believe that he then became deranged as he embarked on the plot that was to bring him to the scaffold, a proposed coup in which he would capture the Queen, force her to dismiss his enemies, and allow him to take over the running of the country. The coup was set to take place on 8 February 1601. So sure was he that he would succeed that he commissioned a special performance of Shakespeare's *Richard II* to be performed at the Globe Theatre. The choice was very specific, dealing as it does with Richard's forced abdication in favour of his enemy, Henry Bolingbroke. Totally unaware of the implications, Burbage duly agreed to the Earl's request.

Yet it seems there had always been a difficulty with regard to *Richard II*, for it had proved so unpopular with the Queen that Richard's great deposition scene, when he is forced to hand the crown to his cousin and enemy, Henry Bolingbroke, was removed from all three versions of the play published during her lifetime. Giving evidence after the event, the actor Augustine Phillips said: 'Sir Charles Percy, Sir Jocelyn Percy and the Lord Mounteagle, with some three more, spoke to some of the players to have the play of the deposing and killing of Richard II to be played, promising them forty shillings more than their ordinary to play it.' Then, in an effort to extricate himself, he added: 'Where this examinate and his fellows were determined to have played some other play, holding the play of King Richard to be old and so long out of use that they should have small or no company at it. But at their request this examinate and his fellows were content to play it the Saturday.' And play it they did, to a packed house.

News of the performance soon reached the Privy Council and Essex was summoned to appear before them at once. He never arrived. The following morning he marched on Whitehall at the head of three hundred swordsmen, despite the attempts of the Lord Chief Justice to prevent him. But this time there were no cheering crowds at the roadside and no one rose up to join him. Within hours he and his closest allies had fled to his house and barricaded themselves in, finally surrendering to Lord Nottingham and Sir Henry Sidney after they had threatened to blow up the house with everyone in it.

The Lord Chamberlain's Men now found themselves in a frightening situation. It was common knowledge that when the Queen had learned of the performance of *Richard II* she had raged, in fury, '*I* am Richard II, know ye not that?' She then went on to state, wrongly, that 'this tragedy was played some forty times in open streets and houses'. The actors must have waited in a state of dread as the Earl and his closest allies were brought to trial by their peers. Essex's partiality to the play was brought up at his trial, that he was 'often present at the playing thereof . . . and with great applause giving countenance and liking to the same'. Potentially awful consequences now stared the company in the face: writers and actors had suffered imprisonment and worse, and playhouses had been closed down, for far less.

Essex and six of his closest associates were found guilty and duly executed. As might be expected of one who never lacked panache, he went to his death exquisitely dressed and with great dignity. He was just thirty-three years old. On the morning of his execution the Queen was in her chamber playing the virginals, when a messenger entered to tell her that the sentence on Essex had been carried out. Nobody spoke. Then the Queen turned back to her instrument and took up the melody at exactly the point where she had left off.

That no further action was actually taken against Shakespeare, Burbage and the rest of company can only be because they had such a powerful patron as the Lord Chamberlain, who could speak on their behalf and assure both the Queen and the Privy Council that they had put on the performance of *Richard II* in all innocence, quite unaware of its implications and certainly without any knowledge of Essex's coup, and be believed. But it had been an extremely close-run thing.

Within two years all was to change with the death of the Queen on 24 March 1603. Tudor chronicler William Camden wrote: 'She was a Queen who hath so long and with so great wisdom governed her kingdoms as (to use the word of her Successor who in sincerity confessed so much) the like have not been read or heard of, either in our own time or since the days of the Roman Emperor Augustus.' The age of Gloriana had passed and the arrival of James VI of Scotland, now James I of England, heralded a new era, a new Court and new ways. It also ushered in a spate of new writing from the biting satirical 'City' comedies to the blood-soaked revenge dramas forever associated with the Jacobeans.

TEN

Jacobean Players and Patrons

It is not everyone's work. The State of Hell must care
Whom it employs in point of reputation,
Here about in London.

Ben Jonson, *The Devil's an Ass*, I, i

The accession of James to the throne was greeted at first with general relief. At last the years of uncertainty over the succession were finally over and the fact that he was now King of both England and Scotland should end the centuries of antagonism and warfare between the two countries; it was also hoped that the new era would put an end to the intrigue and in-fighting at Court. But this optimism did not last long. Whatever people might have thought of Elizabeth, whether they loved or loathed her, she had offered them strong leadership. It was soon obvious that the same could not be said of King James as it became apparent that the country was ruled by a weak, superstitious and wildly extravagant monarch described as 'the wisest fool in Christendom'.

The son of a mother he had not seen since infancy and who was considered by some to be a notorious adulteress who had colluded in the murder of his father, Darnley, and by others as a Catholic martyr, he had hardly had a good start. He had grown up pulled this way and that by the various factions at the Scottish Court and was already showing a preference for young male favourites. By the time he arrived in London for the coronation, his Queen, Anne, had given him two sons and a daughter and during the next two years gave birth to two further daughters, neither of whom survived. But at least she had secured the succession, after which it is suggested that there was no longer any physical relationship between the two, so allowing James to devote himself to the pretty young men on whom he lavished not only his affections but vast sums of money.

'The lowering of standards in the court was immediate', writes Una Ellis-Fermor in *The Jacobean Drama*; 'slackness, loss of dignity and increase of expense combined to produce at once dissatisfaction and a feeling of unsteadiness. Plots to depose him (King James) broke out again almost at once, the first as early as 1603 to be followed by the Gunpowder Plot in 1605.' Whether or not it is true that Robert Cecil, who had been instrumental in securing James's succession to the English throne, had an *agent provocateur* among the Gunpowder Plotters is still a matter of dispute but certainly from then on 'Papists' were hunted with fanatical zeal. Aware that he owed Cecil a great deal, James created him first Viscount Cranborne in 1604 then, in 1605, Earl of Salisbury. The Gunpowder Plot had confirmed his worst fears and given his suspicion of anything remotely Catholic, his belief in spells and witchcraft, and his ability to take offence at anything he considered to be remotely critical of himself or his entourage, it would seem that the professional life of a dramatist was likely to be every bit as hazardous as it had been during Elizabeth's last years.

His Court was rotten with graft and corruption. It seemed that everything was now for sale. It was no longer just the King's favourites on whom honours were lavished, and soon James and his advisers had thought up a truly splendid way of filling the country's coffers: selling titles. Much of today's nobility who have (or until recently had) seats in the House of Lords owe their status and rank to the fact that an early seventeenth-century ancestor had plenty of ready cash. At the bottom end of the scale for a mere £30 you could buy yourself a knighthood, and so many young men were eager to take advantage of this that the country soon boasted no less than 838 new knights. If you were more ambitious and had more money to spare, then £1,905 would buy you the new rank of knight baronet. Within a comparatively short time the King had created three new dukes, a marquess, no less than *thirty* earls, nineteen viscounts and fifty-six barons, all strictly for cash in hand, the final total of which is estimated to have been in the region of £120,000. If you could get away with it, it is obvious that such a situation was ripe for exploitation on the stage.

Disillusion became general. The anonymous commentator quoted at the beginning of the chapter continues: 'for in London their brother shall die in the streets for cold, he shall lie sick at the door between stock and stock . . . and perish there for hunger. . . . When any (rich) man died, they would bequeath great sums of money to the poor, but now I hear no good report, and yet inquire of it, and hearken for it; but now charity is waxen cold, non helpeth the scholar, nor yet the poor.'[1]

However one of the immediate beneficiaries of the new reign was the company of the Lord Chamberlain's Men. James enjoyed plays and masques and almost straight away became their personal patron, the seal of royal approval giving them the title of the King's Men, Henslowe's company and those of the Earls of Oxford and Worcester later coming under the patronage of the Queen and Prince. We know that the King's Men were asked to perform at Court as part of King James's very first Christmas festivities and that the company performed *Measure for Measure* on Boxing Day and *Love's Labour's Lost* and 'the play of Errors' over the following days. If that seems quite a heavy schedule, director Gregory Doran, in his foreword to a new edition of the play *Eastward Ho!* points out that, according to *Henslowe's Diary* during the 1594/5 season at the Rose Theatre, the Lord Admiral's Men performed thirty-eight plays, twenty-one of which were new. There was no such thing as a long run of a popular play; audiences expected a different play to be performed every day.

Apart from George Chapman, Shakespeare was now by far the most senior and established survivor of the handful of playwrights who had come to prominence in the late 1580s and early 1590s, for the turn of the century had seen the death of two of the remaining University Wits, George Peele and Thomas Nashe. In neither case is the date of their demise certain. Peele probably died some time around 1598–9 although he was credited with *Merry Conceited Jests of George Peele, Gentleman* as late as 1605. Francis Meres wrote in his *Wit's Treasury* that Peele died of 'a loathsome disease', which might well have been true since he drank heavily and slept around. Nashe almost certainly died in 1601 and various suggestions have been put forward as to the cause, since he was only thirty-four years old, including plague or a stroke. An anonymous tribute to him says:

> Let all his faults sleep with his mournful chest,
> And there for ever with his ashes rest.
> His style was witty, though it had some gall,
> Some things he might have mended, so may all.
> Yet this I say, that for a mother wit,
> Few men have ever seen the like of it.

But whatever their faults, Jacobean Londoners were keen playgoers, writers remained in great demand and there was plenty of work to choose from. Records show that a mixture of familiar and new works were produced in 1604 including Shakespeare's *Measure for Measure* and *Othello*. *Macbeth*, widely considered to be a compliment to James's ancestry and his expertise on the subject of witchcraft, is generally dated a little later. There was also Chapman's *Bussy d'Ambois* (a rather dull historical piece), and his *All Fools*; *The Honest Whore* by Dekker and the emergent John Webster, who possibly also wrote *The Play of Sir Thomas Wyatt*; *Westward Ho!*, another Dekker collaboration; Heywood's *If You Know Not Me You Know Nobody* and Marston's *The Wise Woman of Hogsden*, *The Malcontent* and the intriguing *The Dutch Courtesan*; and Cyril Tourneur's *The Atheist's Tragedy*. Tourneur is a somewhat shadowy figure whose father spent his life in the service of the Cecil family and there is a strong suggestion that he, like Marlowe, was recruited into the secret service. He is best known for the splendid *Revenger's Tragedy*, although some academics now want to credit Middleton with its authorship.[2]

One reason for the doubts over its provenance is that Tourneur's manuscripts, along with many others from the same period, were later destroyed by 'Warburton's cook' some time in the eighteenth century. Sir John Warburton, who lived from 1682 to 1759, was an avid collector of almost anything, including old manuscripts, and over the years had managed to obtain the original 'books' of a number of Elizabethan and Jacobean playwrights, including some of those of Jonson and Middleton which are now recorded only as 'lost plays'. He lived hard, drank heavily and unfortunately failed to look after his acquisitions properly. In 1729, to keep himself in drink, he sold one batch of manuscripts to the Earl of Oxford but later most of his collection of rare plays was, through the ignorance of his servant and cook, Betty Baker, 'unluckily burned or put under pie bottoms . . .' and a list of some fifty-five 'lost plays' exists in his own handwriting.

True to his promise Jonson had devoted himself to tragedy and written *Sejanus*, set in the period of Tiberius Caesar. Anne Barton in her biography of Jonson writes that it was a play he wrote very much to please himself but also to 'demonstrate how a Roman tragedy ought to be composed'.[3] He actually presented his script to the King's Men in 1603 but it does not seem to have been greeted with much enthusiasm and it was some time before it was put on. Anne Barton suggests that Shakespeare himself might well have insisted on cuts and rewriting – after all he was not only the house playwright and a shareholder but likely to be acting in it; if so, even he was unable to make a success of it when it was finally staged at the Globe. It did not go down well with audiences. Jonson was furious and blamed the King's Men, going so far, when he later had *Sejanus* published, as to describe the script as played as 'a ruin' that had 'suffered no less violence from our people here, then the subject of it did from the rage of the people of Rome', pointing out that his tragedy had been torn limb from limb as had his protagonist. Nor, to add insult to injury, was that the end of the matter, for he was then hauled before the Privy Council to answer a charge of Popery in the acting text, although he seems to have been able to satisfy the authorities on that score and the matter was dropped, which is possibly why he thought it safer to return to comedy.

Eastward Ho! was commissioned from Jonson's old antagonist, John Marston, in 1605 for the company of the Children of her Majesty's Revels, a company of boy actors of which he was a shareholder. Obviously the two had made up their differences for the subsequent script was the result of a collaboration between Marston, Jonson and the older and more experienced George Chapman.

Its underlying theme, one which was to prove very popular with Jacobean dramatists, is the gaining and acquisition of wealth and what people will do to obtain it. In this case it is 'Sir Petronel Flash' who is to marry Gertrude, the daughter of a wealthy goldsmith, solely for her money. Her father encourages the match, believing that he is buying not only into the nobility but into even more wealth. Both are to be disappointed. Towards the end of the play after a series of adventures, most of the main protagonists arrive at the Blue Anchor Tavern, presumably situated in a dockland area like Deptford, having decided to try their luck in the New World whither they are bound in a vessel captained by one Captain Seagull.

After a heavy night on the drink the adventurers duly set off on their epic voyage but are shipwrecked almost straightaway. The first survivors are convinced that they have been stranded on the French coast. Cold, wet and having lost all their money and possessions they finally attract the attention of two passers-by who are addressed by their reluctant spokesman in an early version of Franglais, only to discover that the shore on which they stand is not the coast of France but that of the Isle of Dogs: their ship had never even left the shelter of the Thames. It is during the exchange when their situation is made clear to them that disparaging remarks are made about 'the King's thirty pound knights' and dim Scotsmen. No doubt the audience thought it hilarious. But not everyone was laughing. Sir James Murray, one of the King's favourites who had gone to see the play, was enraged at what he considered a gross insult to the King and his nobility, not to mention all Scotsmen, and immediately complained to James who promptly ordered the arrest of all three playwrights.

How fortunate it is then that Jonson was later able to give his own version of subsequent events to William Drummond, who duly recorded the story. He had much to record, for Jonson had invited himself to stay with Drummond in his Scottish home, where he spent night after night talking about himself. According to Drummond,

Jonson told him that he was not arrested but 'voluntarily' imprisoned himself with Chapman and Marston, who had been thrust into gaol for 'writing something against the Scots in a play, *Eastward Ho!*', and that he had chosen to share their fate when he learned 'the report was that they should have their ears cut and noses'. Further, that after the three were finally released from prison (without injury), at a subsequent feast to celebrate his homecoming, Jonson's 'old mother drank to him and showed . . . a paper which she had (if the sentence had taken execution) to have mixed in the prison among his drink, which was full of lusty poison, and that she was no churl, she told him, for she minded first to have drunk of it herself'.[4]

This moving anecdote, that Jonson had 'voluntarily' gone to prison with his mates, and that his dear old mum was prepared to poison both herself and him rather than that he should suffer the disgrace of having his nose and ears slit, was believed right up to 1901 when letters from Chapman and Jonson, addressed to various members of the nobility during their time in prison, were discovered in a collection of seventeenth-century manuscripts owned by a Mr T.A. White of New York. From these it was discovered that the reality was, to say the least, somewhat different. For a start Marston never went to prison at all, nor is there any suggestion that Jonson 'volunteered' to go to gaol: he had no option. Once incarcerated, so far from playing the swaggering hero with the noble mother, he spent his entire time writing obsequious letters to various titled people pleading with them to get him out.

One of these was addressed to 'The Most Noble Virtuous and Thrice-Honoured Earl of Salisbury', Robert Cecil himself, in which Jonson informs him:

> I am here, most honoured Lord, unexamined and unheard, committed to a vile prison, and with me a gentleman (whose name may perhaps have come to your Lordship), one, Mr. George Chapman, a learned and honest man. The cause (would I could name some worthier, though I wish we had known none worthy of imprisonment), is (the word irks me that our fortunes have necessitated us to so despised a course) a play, my Lord.

After much more in similar vein he concludes:

But lest I be too diligent for my excuse that I may incur the suspicion of being guilty, I become a most humble suitor to your Lordship that with the honourable Lord Chamberlain (to whom I have in like manner petitioned), you will be the grateful means of our coming answer; or if in your wisdom it shall be thought unnecessary, that your Lordship will be the most honoured cause of our liberty. Where freeing us from one prison you shall remove us to another; which is eternally to bind us and our muses, to the thankful honouring of you and yours to posterity; as your own virtues have by many descents of ancestors ennobled you to time. Your Honour's most devoted in heart and words – Ben Jonson

Whether it was his sycophantic letters or Chapman's more restrained correspondence that finally brought about their release is not known, but by the beginning of October 1605 they had both been freed. Nor is it recorded anywhere that Jonson threw the party at which his aged mother is alleged to have waved a paper of poison at the assembled throng. However, it is known that on 9 October he did attend one. It was a party given by Robert Catesby, one of the conspirators in the Gunpowder Plot, which was timed to take place just under four weeks later.[5]

The first decade of the seventeenth century also saw a new and major development on the theatre scene. As early as 1595 when the Burbages and the Lord Chamberlain's Men were still based at the original Theatre on the north side of the Thames, James Burbage had felt the need to expand. At that stage he had no plans to move his main enterprise south to the Bankside but he was already having trouble with the freeholder and must have considered the possibility that at some stage he might well have to do so. What he had in mind now, however, was something quite different, a theatre building which was not dependent on the weather and offered its audiences more comfort. Since these two factors alone meant that he would be able to charge more for admittance, such a venue would surely be very profitable. He decided therefore, when he was offered the opportunity, to buy a large and imposing building in the fashionable district of Blackfriars and convert it into a 'private', i.e. covered, theatre. It was, as Gurr says, to be 'an emphatic shift upmarket'.

The building had been part of the old monastery of the Black Friars which Henry VIII, on the Dissolution of the Monasteries, had handed over to his then Master of Revels. It had a continuing theatrical connection, for in the 1570s it was used by the Master of the Children of the Chapel Royal for storage, possibly, rehearsals and also for a certain number of performances, but by the 1590s it was mostly let out for lodgings. It seemed to the Burbages to be the ideal venue, fashionably situated with a wealthy audience within convenient strolling distance, yet easily reached from the south side of the river.

But apparently the wealthy citizens of Blackfriars did not relish the idea of a new centre of culture in their midst and petitioned the Privy Council to forbid its use on the grounds that:

> It will be a great annoyance and trouble, not only to all the noblemen and gentlemen here inhabiting but also a general inconvenience to all the inhabitants of the same precinct, both by reason of the great resort and gathering together of all manner of vagrant and lewd persons that, under colour of resorting to the players, will come thither and work all manner of mischief, and also to the great pestering and filling up of the same precinct . . . and besides, that the same playhouse is so near the Church that the noise of the drums and trumpets will greatly disturb and hinder both the ministers and parishioners in time of divine service and sermons.

This sounds like nothing so much as an objection to an application today to open a nightclub. James Burbage had hoped that, as the Lord Chamberlain himself lived nearby, he would have pressed their case, but he was to be disappointed for, as the Privy Councillor responsible for the playhouses, Henry Carey signed the order preventing the change of use for the building to go ahead. It was necessary therefore to shelve the whole plan and anyway by 1599 the Burbages and the Lord Chamberlain's Men were fully occupied rebuilding and reopening the remains of the old Theatre on the Bankside as the new Globe.

On the death of James, Richard inherited the building on which they had tried to recoup some of their expenditure by letting out sections of it. Yet it would seem that parts of the building were used after that by the Blackfriars Boys, one of the popular 'boy companies' who gained a reputation in the early 1600s for performing satirical comedies, and that the local people had no objection to that. Whether it was because there was no precedent or their neighbours had changed their minds, in 1608 Burbage was finally granted permission to go ahead. The opening of a second venue meant that he now had far more flexibility. Soon the Blackfriars was joined by other new theatres. North of the river, the Boar's Head in Whitechapel was added to the Curtain (still in use after all these years) while Henslowe had built a second theatre, the Hope (which also doubled as a bear pit), on the site of the old Bear Garden close to the Globe and the Swan.

With their establishment in the Blackfriars Theatre Burbage's company, as Gurr points out, 'with their kingly title and unique repertoire of Shakespeare's plays became the outstanding company in every way, whether they were performing at the Blackfriars or the Globe'. Their pre-eminence as the King's Men no doubt encouraged the company to undertake the 'extravagance' of maintaining two playhouses. It gave the company real flexibility. They could play in the Globe in the summer, where it was possible to pack in an audience of three thousand and thus maximise their profits, and in the winter, or if the weather was bad, in the new theatre where both players and audience were protected from the elements, which meant there was far less chance in future of having to cancel performances. From now on the company, if it wished, could play six afternoons a week.

ELEVEN

Roaring Girls

... it pleased our Lord and Saviour, Jesus Christ, without the
assistance of man ... from the time of his conception to be
begotten of a woman, born of a woman, nourished by a woman
... he healed women, pardoned women, comforted women ...
                    Emilia Lanier, *The Virtuous Reader* (1611)

Women are noticeably absent from the theatrical world of the
Elizabethans and Jacobeans in no small part because, unlike
the situation in Catholic Spain or the Italian states where it was
considered a perfectly respectable profession, in England it was still
against the law for a woman to appear on stage. Presumably their
only professional contact with the players' companies was as
seamstresses making, repairing or cleaning costumes and laundering
what was washable. That they were not allowed to perform is
somewhat ironic as, throughout the period when the prohibition
was in force, wealthy ladies could regularly disport themselves in
court masques, often in a daring range of costumes, without in any
way damaging their reputations. When, after the Restoration,
women were finally allowed into the acting profession, the term
'actress' was virtually synonymous with that of 'whore'.

So, as we know, women's roles were played by the boys until their
voices broke and it must have added to the comedy of situations
such as that of Viola in *Twelfth Night* and Rosalind in *As You Like
It* to see a boy playing a girl masquerading as a boy. But it is often
asked how such young lads could possibly have coped with roles
such as those of Lady Macbeth and Cleopatra or, indeed, Beatrice-
Joanna in *The Changeling*. But having seen Mark Rylance's all male
productions at today's Globe, one wonders if that might not also

have been a possibility in the late sixteenth and early seventeenth centuries. Not to mention the possibility that a character like the nurse in *Romeo and Juliet* might have been played by a middle-aged actor as a kind of pantomime dame as in the film *Shakespeare in Love*. What we do know is that on the other hand, apart from rare exceptions such as Nathan Field, the boy actors did not successfully make the transition to male roles.

Of the women who were actually involved with our playwrights and actors we know hardly anything, which is scarcely surprising as the dramatists themselves merit little in the way of contemporary biographical information unless, like Marlowe, they ended up spectacularly dead. The exception is Ben Jonson, who was a great self-publicist but had little or nothing to say about the women in his life. We know that Shakespeare's mother was considered sufficiently capable by her father to be left the family estate but Anne Hathaway will remain forever a shadowy figure, and it seems unlikely that there will ever be agreement as to the identity of the Dark Lady of the Sonnets. Of his daughters we know that Susannah was literate, respectable and married a doctor and that Judith was probably illiterate, not at all respectable, and married Quiney's son, a marriage which proved anything but happy. Then there is poor Emma Ball (and her ironically named lovechild, Fortunatus), mistress first to Tarlton, then to Robert Greene who lived off her, then treated her so badly, as indeed he did the flaxen-haired wife he had married for money, while Jonson dismissed his wife, the mother of his children, as an honest shrew. Middleton had a strong-minded mother, older sisters and an educated wife from a good family but we know nothing more about her than that.

As for the actors, a 'Mistress Burbage' who might well have been Richard's wife (although it cannot be proved) consulted Forman on both health and astrological matters in the 1590s, and we know something of Edward Alleyn's wife Joan through their surviving correspondence. They were obviously fond of each other but the marriage was childless and when she died he swiftly took another, much younger wife, the daughter of the poet and divine, John Donne. We also know, apart from the anecdote featuring William the

Conqueror and Richard III, that much like today good-looking and charismatic actors had no shortage of offers even from 'respectable' women. But apart from the Dark Lady, it is impossible to know how much any of their relationships influenced the writers concerned.

From various official records and lists of trades we know that there were extremely efficient women who, if their husbands were away for a considerable time or had left them widowed, were quite capable of running the family business. Also, from the Forman diaries it is clear that, at least throughout the 1590s, women from the merchant class or those married to successful artisans had a considerable amount of freedom and relative independence. But to be recorded in the histories of the late Elizabethan or early Jacobean age, unless you committed a really serious crime or were tried for witchcraft, you needed to be aristocratic, eccentric, notorious or all three for history to remember you. For instance Mary Herbert, a noted wit, was the Earl of Pembroke's second wife (his first had been Catherine Grey, the sister of Lady Jane Grey) and Sir Philip Sidney's sister. She and her brother were very close (he dedicated his *Arcadia* to her) and had been pupils of Dr Dee, inspiring in Mary a lasting interest in mathematics and the new sciences, so much so that she later had her own laboratory. Then there is the stunningly beautiful courtesan Venetia Stanley, who drove men mad and who expected any lover to lavish a fortune on her in the way of clothes and jewels, while for both high status and notoriety there is Frances Howard, Countess of Essex, best known for wrecking her marriage to the Earl by falling in love with King James's favourite, James Carr, alongside whom she later stood trial for the murder of Sir Thomas Overbury.

Parents of girls born into comfortably off families had always been seen as marriage bargains, but from the commentators of the time it does seem that the position of such girls and women after James came to the throne worsened. They became, like the knighthoods and baronetcies, saleable commodities. Ambitious fathers rushed to take their pretty daughters to Court, wealthy businessmen sought out the newly ennobled, offering cash in exchange for status, all of which provided the dramatists with material for the new 'city comedies' and 'satires' which were proving so popular. Women with any position at Court easily acquired doubtful reputations. Commentators thundered against the morals of both sexes but most especially the women since, as is ever the case, double standards applied. Of the Queen's own ladies the Earl of Worcester wrote: 'the plotting and malice amongst them is such that I think envy hath tied an invisible snake about most of their necks to sting one another to death'. It was a place full of 'persons betraying and betrayed'. They, too, provided role models for a new wave of writing.

However, for those at the bottom of the heap, life was hard indeed. At the turn of the century the average wage was about seven pence a day in old money, even less for agricultural labourers and the unskilled. Wage rates were set by the justices, and employers who paid more could actually be sent to prison; thus a significant proportion of the population lived below the poverty line and, as always in such circumstances, some women turned to prostitution, especially those who through no fault of their own found themselves unemployed and penniless; the Jacobean Court attracted pimps and procuresses in droves, only too eager to run professional operations in this new and merciless commercial world. Marston in his play *The Dutch Courtesan* presents just such a character in the Mistress of the Brothel. During a discussion on various types of city trade and who is presently making the most money, she points out that in strictly financial terms hers is the most soundly based trade of all as there is always a demand for 'such divine virtues as virginity, modesty and such rare gems', which she now sells 'not like a petty chapman, by retail, but like a great merchant, by wholesale'. Outside the orbit of such professionals, there were the hundreds of freelancers who operated like Dr Forman's 'Julia in Seething Lane', possibly taking clients home, more often accommodating them up against a wall in an alley. Child prostitution too was rife and there was little attempt at concealment. The young rake, Sir Pexall Brockas, is said to have 'owned a young mignon . . . whom he had entertained and abused since she was twelve years old'.

Women before or since have rarely had a worse press. Misogynists and moralists had a field day, among them the King himself, whose general distaste for the female sex led him to order the clergy 'to inveigh vehemently against the insolency of our women'. Joseph Swetnam in his cumbersomely entitled *The Arraignment of Lewd, Idle, Forward and Unconstant Women: Or the Vanity of Them: Choose you Whether* writes: 'Moses describeth a woman thus: "At the first beginning a woman was made to be a helper unto man", and so they are indeed: for she helpeth to spend and consume that which man painfully getteth.' Later, after stating that most women are only after money, he continues: '. . . but if thy pockets grow empty, and thy revenues will not hold out longer to maintain her pomp and bravery, then she presently leaves to make much of thy person, and will not stick to say unto thee that she could have bestowed her love on such a one as would have maintained her like a woman.'

It is therefore hardly surprising that the female characters in the Jacobean plays, with few exceptions, fall into recognisable categories reflecting, the writers might have said, the general attitude towards women in the society of the day. Shakespeare is exceptional, his female characters throughout the canon of thirty-eight plays unique. From Queen Margaret, the tigress of the early *Henry VI* plays, through to the naive Miranda of *The Tempest*, taking in en route women as diverse as Kate, Juliet, Viola, Beatrice, Isabella, Lady Macbeth, Cressida, Desdemona, Cleopatra, Hermione and Paulina, Shakespeare's women are very much themselves, no one of them is like another and almost all, during the course of the action, are changed by the experiences they undergo during the course of the action. They are real people who one feels had a life before the play began and, if they survive, one that continues after the story comes to an end, which is why actresses love to play them.

This might also be said of some of Middleton's women and a handful of others, but on the whole the female roles in Jacobean theatre are stereotypical. Most sympathetic are the feisty like Doll, one of the rogues in Jonson's *The Alchemist*, and the widow in Middleton's *A Trick to Catch the Old One*, who successfully does just that. They are likeable because at least they hold their own in a man's world. Bess, in Heywood's *Fair Maid of the West*, fearing that her lover has been captured by the Spaniards, fits out a ship and takes to the seas as captain of a privateer, a role accepted by the men under her command. Prior to this she has made an example of a swaggering rogue who made a pass at her by disguising herself as a young man and challenging him to a fight which she wins – after which she literally walks all over him. She is that rare thing, a successful woman, and by the end of the play her privateering has proved profitable and she has rescued her lover from Barbary pirates, tactfully avoiding the advances of their leader, Mullisheg. Many sixteenth- and early seventeenth-century women must have enjoyed seeing women portrayed on stage in such a way for in real life there were plenty of independent-minded women. Shakespeare's Merry Wives are based firmly in the world of the Stratford in which he grew up; they are not creatures of fantasy.

But far more women are presented in drama as ever compliant, doing their duty by their fathers, brothers or husbands whatever sacrifice it might entail. In Middleton's *A Chaste Maid in Cheapside* Allwit's wife, at his express order, agrees to become the mistress of filthy rich Sir Walter Whorehound and even bears him a child, Allwit content for the situation to continue indefinitely so long as Sir Walter keeps the money pouring in. Meanwhile in the same play, the character of Touchstone, having passed himself off as a doctor, steps in to rescue the bullied Lady Kix from the apparent infertility which is ruining her marriage as her husband, who can only inherit a fortune if he has an heir and blames her for not providing him with one, goes along with her being impregnated by 'the doctor' under cover of supposed medical treatment.

Then there is woman as victim: we first meet Vendice in *The Revenger's Tragedy* cradling the skull of his fiancée who has been poisoned by the Duke after refusing to sleep with him, and as part of his strategy of revenge persuades his mother to procure his sister for that same Duke. Webster's *Duchess of Malfi* (based on a real event in medieval Italy) is murdered simply for marrying outside her station in life. Having married the first time to please the family, on her husband's death she marries her steward for love, thus bringing down on herself the wrath of her brother who considers she has dishonoured the family name and so must be disposed of. The

Dutch courtesan in Marston's play of that name is the mistress of a young and upwardly mobile Londoner to whom she has been totally faithful. He, however, decides he must make a good marriage if he wants to continue to live the life to which he has become accustomed and to that end hands her over to an unpleasant friend, a character who offers a study in sexual repression and sadism well ahead of its time. At the end of the play the unfortunate woman seeks out her original lover and physically attacks him for what he has exposed her to, as a result of which she is sent to prison for an indefinite time while he marries a pretty young woman with a large dowry. In Heywood's *A Woman Killed with Kindness*, an erring wife is treated by her husband (who considers he is acting from the best of motives) in such a way that she literally dies of shame.

Lastly there are the wicked, scheming, *evil* women: in Beaumont and Fletcher's *The Maid's Tragedy*, Amintor, at the suggestion of the King, has jilted, almost at the altar, the long-suffering Aspatia (yet another victim) in favour of his friend's sister, Evadne. But on his wedding night his Evadne informs him that theirs will be a marriage in name only as she is the King's mistress and that he has married her off so that any child she might bear the King will be born in wedlock. When the King demands to know if she will stay faithful to him she answers that she will – so long as no one even richer and more powerful than he is comes along. Eventually she is persuaded to murder him in a scene worthy of a handbook on strange sexual practices: when she ties him to the bed he assumes it is foreplay for some strange sex game.

However one of the most fascinating women in this genre and an exception to typecasting is Beatrice-Joanna in Middleton and Rowley's *The Changeling*. Having persuaded her steward (long in love with her) to murder her fiancé so that she can marry the man of her choice, she imagines he will be satisfied with being well paid for what he has done: 'Belike his wants are greedy, and to such gold tastes like angels food', she tells herself and the audience. Only after the deed is done does she discover that it is not money he wants but her and that she has no alternative but to give in. Faced then with the prospect of her new husband discovering on the wedding night that she is not a virgin, she embarks on yet more murders, finally having to face at the end of the play that she has indeed become, in the steward's words 'a woman dipped in blood'. *The Changeling* is a great play.

Faced with the confines of the society in which they lived and portrayed in popular entertainment in the way they were, it was a rare soul who not only broke the mould but is actually recorded as having done so. Yet two most unusual women did, in their different ways, manage it. Their lives overlap both the late Elizabethan and Jacobean ages and both are linked in their different ways to theatre and the playhouses. One, just possibly, provided the inspiration for Rosaline in Shakespeare's *Love's Labour's Lost*, the other certainly inspired Middleton and Dekker's play *The Roaring Girl*.

The first, Emilia Lanier née Bassano, came to light during the late Dr A.L. Rowse's search for Shakespeare's Dark Lady of the Sonnets and his conviction that he had finally found her brought down on his head both controversy and derision from a variety of academics during his lifetime, an argument that has raged ever since. It is difficult to understand how his suggestion should have created such animosity since the various previous contenders would appear to be considerably less likely.[1] For a long time the prime favourite was a court lady, Mary Fitton, yet anyone visiting the home of the Newdigate family, Arbury Hall in Warwickshire, will see from the portrait of her which hangs in the picture gallery there that she bears no resemblance whatsoever to Shakespeare's lady whose hair, we are told, was like 'black wires' and who had dark eyes and dun-coloured skin. Mary Fitton's hair is red-gold and she has blue/grey eyes and a white complexion, though she was certainly promiscuous enough to fill the role, taking several lovers at Court before running off to Plymouth to live with a privateer. The Arbury portrait is quite eerie for it shows her wearing a magnificent brocade dress which appears to be crawling with spiders, beetles and other insects.

Dr Rowse 'found' Emilia in the Simon Forman manuscripts in the Bodleian Library in Oxford. Forman, with whom Emilia had a brief affair, described her at the time of their liaison as having been 'very brave' (that is, dashing) 'in her youth'. The Bassano family originated in Venice, coming to England towards the end of the reign of Henry VIII, and they must have been talented for they were soon Court musicians. Emilia was the daughter of Baptisto Bassano and his common-law wife Margaret Johnston, and the family lived in the parish of St Botolph in Bishopsgate alongside many theatre people with whom they must certainly have become acquainted. In 1576 Bassano died leaving two daughters, Angela and Emilia, who was only six. By 7 July 1586, when Margaret Johnston died, Angela had long been married to Joseph Holland, 'gentleman', and Emilia, just seventeen, was on her own.

Her father had left her £100 in his will, to be paid to her either at the age of twenty-one or when she married – but as she did not fancy any of the men who were offered for her, this meant a four-year wait. So what was there for an intelligent, ambitious girl with neither background nor money who did not want either to go into ordinary service or marry the first man who came along? Emilia was nothing if not pragmatic. A third option was that of the kept woman. She was aware she had undoubted gifts; her dark good looks were attractive to men, she was a talented musician in her own right and was fluent in Italian. But being a kept woman by any man who could afford her was not enough; her aim was to go to Court, which she did by finding employment in the household of the Countess of Kent. The countess took Emilia with her to Court where her undoubted musical ability brought her into the public eye, for she was sufficiently proficient at the virginals to play for the Queen, no mean practitioner herself.

It was then that she caught the eye of Henry Carey, Lord Hunsdon, the Lord Chamberlain, who was old enough to be her grandfather but who was by that time (the early 1590s) the patron of Burbage's company, the Lord Chamberlain's Men. One of the reasons for believing that she might have been the Dark Lady is that if she was not acquainted with Shakespeare before she became involved with his patron, then she must certainly have met him after for he was also an actor and would have taken part in performances not only in the playhouse but at private parties given by the Lord

Chamberlain and also, as we know from the records, at Court. But there is unlikely ever to be proof.

From what she later told Forman, the Lord Chamberlain was very generous to his young mistress, keeping her in great style and lavishing on her both jewels and money. She remained his mistress for some time, but all good things come to an end and in spite of the disparity in their ages she became pregnant by him, or claimed that she had. Much as Henry VIII had married off his own mistress, Mary Boleyn, to William Carey, his son Henry Carey arranged a marriage for Emilia with another court musician, Alfonso Lanier. He was three years younger than she was and neither pretended it was anything else but a marriage of convenience. Her son by Carey, baptised Henry after his father, later became a Court musician to Charles I. Forman describes her situation bluntly: 'She was paramour to old Lord Hunsdon that was Lord Chamberlain and maintained by him in great pride; then, being with child, she was for colour married to a minstrel.' She told Forman that she did not reckon much to the bargain that had been made for her.

It is hardly surprising therefore that, soon bored with her husband, she took lovers, but if Forman's experience is anything to go by, she led them a merry dance. Over a period of weeks she consulted him on both medical and astrological matters. Regarding the latter she wanted to know if Alfonso, who somewhat surprisingly had gone off with the Earl of Essex on his venture to Cadiz, was likely to survive the voyage and return home. Forman told her that he would; also that it was unlikely that he would ever achieve much or bring her wealth or improved status (she had dreams of being a titled lady). It is hard to decide, from Forman's account, which of them then made the first move but after some dalliance during visits to him in his consulting room, she invited him back to her place for supper. But he was to discover, when he eagerly took up her invitations, that even if the evening ended with her inviting him into her bed, he did not necessarily always have what he wanted. She would grant him much, take off her clothes and invite him to fondle any part of her body willingly 'but then would not do it in any wise'. Finally, frustrated and cross, he had had enough and the affair ended. This certainly has overtones of the Dark Lady who was also, if the Sonnets are to be believed, a considerable sexual tease.

Her career up till then is not all unusual, other than the fact that her existence is at least recorded. It was when she was older and had possibly given up men that she became known for something altogether different. She reinvented herself as a poet. Although written considerably earlier, Shakespeare's Sonnets were first published in 1609, her own in 1611. Just as the male poets and dramatists had acquired patrons, so too did Emilia and her poems are dedicated to, among others, the Queen, Arabella Stewart, Susan, Dowager Countess of Kent, and the Countesses of Suffolk, Cumberland and Dorset.

It cannot be said in truth that Emilia was a good poet. What makes her work of considerable interest is that in her poetry she puts up a stout defence of women and their place in the scheme of things, especially those she considers have been treated unfairly by history. She begins at the beginning with Eve. Eve, she writes, was deceived by cunning and intended no harm when she handed Adam the apple to eat. Indeed it was more fool him for taking it:

> But surely Adam cannot be excused
> Her fault, though great, yet he was most to blame;
> What weakness offered, strength might have refused,
> Being Lord of All, the greater was his shame:
> Although the serpent's craft had her abused,
> God's Holy Word ought all his actions frame,
> For he was Lord and King of all the earth,
> Before poor Eve had either life or breath.

In the classical world both Helen of Troy and Lucrece are excused for what they did on account of the fact that it was their beauty that drove men wild. They should have controlled themselves better. Therefore it was not Helen's fault that Paris abducted her and started the Trojan War or that Lucrece was raped by Tarquin. As for Cleopatra, history has treated her as unfairly as it has Fair Rosamund. Emilia has a soft spot for Cleopatra and in an essay by

Rowse, *The Poems of Shakespeare's Dark Lady*, he quotes a letter from Agatha Christie saying that she felt that Emilia would dearly have loved to play the part of Cleopatra on stage herself. Then there are her 'heroines', Sisera who hammered a nail through the head of Jael, and Judith who decapitated Holofernes, alongside other strong-minded Biblical women such as Deborah and Susannah.

All this is carefully framed in a Christian context, however, since Emilia obviously did not wish to upset her various patrons. Never having achieved the title of Lady Lanier, she remained keenly aware of her own status, yet in a poem dedicated to Lady Anne Clifford, Countess of Dorset, she points out delicately that one cannot choose the rank into which one is born:

> For how doth Gentry come to rise and fall?
> Or who is he that very rightly can
> Distinguish of his birth, or tell at all
> In what mean state his ancestors have been,
> Before some one of worth did honour win?

Most striking of all is her preface to 'The Virtuous Reader', surely an early example of feminist writing whether or not Emilia would have considered herself as such:

As also in respect it pleased our Lord and Saviour, Jesus Christ, without the assistance of man, being free from original and other sins from the time of his conception, till the hour of his death, to be begotten of a woman, born of a woman, nourished by a woman, obedient to a woman; and that he healed women, pardoned women, comforted women; yea, even when he was in his greatest agony and bloody sweat, going to be crucified, and also in the last hour of his death, took care to dispose of a woman: after his resurrection, appeared first to a woman, then sent a woman to declare his most glorious resurrection to the rest of the Disciples.

A remarkable lady, Emilia. We know little of her subsequent career except that she fell out with her landlord, an army officer, refusing to leave her house when he returned from Europe and wanted it back. There followed three years of court cases before she finally left in the August of 1619 without paying her last quarter's rent and deliberately leaving the house 'in great decay and a nasty, filthy state'. She lived to become a grandmother and great-grandmother and died in 1645 at the age of seventy-six.

Sometime in 1608 or early 1609 playgoers attending a performance at the Fortune Theatre were treated to a new comedy by Thomas Dekker and Thomas Middleton: *The Roaring Girl*. The title itself was amusing since the adjective was one normally applied to noisy, swaggering, roistering men. But this particular play was most unusual in that its protagonist was not only a real person but one very well known to those living on the Bankside and even beyond, for by the time the play was put on she had achieved a considerable reputation.[2]

  Mary or 'Moll' Frith, the daughter of a London shoemaker, 'a fair and square-conditioned man', was born in 1584. A brief biography is given in a pamphlet written not long after her death, *The Life and Death of Mrs. Mary Frith, commonly called Mal Cutpurse exactly collected and now published for the delights and recreations of all merry disposed persons*. Although born into a very similar background to the playwrights and players among whom she socialised there was, of course, no question of the grammar school education that had been so vital to them, but the pamphlet notes that:

particular care was expended on her education, for her boisterous and masculine spirit caused her parents much solicitude. A very Tomrigg and Rumpscuttle she was and delighted and sported in boys' play and pastimes, not minding the company of girls; many a blow and bang this hoyting procured her, but she was not so to be tamed or taken off from her rude inclinations.

  She could not endure the sedentary life of sewing and stitching, her needle, bodkin and thimble, she could not think on quietly, wishing them changed to a sword or a dagger and cudgels; working a sampler was as grievous as stitching a winding sheet. She would fight the boys and courageously beat them, run, jump, leap and hop with any of them or any other play whatsoever.

Came the time, when Moll reached the age of fifteen or sixteen, that she was expected to repay her parents' care and teaching and make a suitable match, and a number of likely husbands were suggested to her. The prospect did not appeal, for 'household work of any kind was distasteful to her and above all she had an abhorrence to the tending of children, to whom she ever had an aversion in her mind equal to the sterility of her womb, never being made a mother to the best of our information'.

The latter may or may not have been true but certainly at the age of sixteen she ran away from home and embarked on what was considered a wildly exotic and eccentric lifestyle, dressing in men's clothes when she felt like it, smoking a pipe and practising her skill with the rapier until she became an expert swordswoman. She was also an excellent shot. She set up home on the Bankside and mixed freely with the Bankside underclass and low life as well as theatre people and was roundly condemned by the authorities as 'a bully, whore, bawd, pickpurse, fortune-teller, receiver and forger', much of which was untrue. She was never a whore. There have been suggestions that she was gay or bisexual but her two long-term relationships were with men, 'the notorious Captain Hind, highwayman' and 'one, Richard Hannam, a worthy who constantly wore a watchmaker and jeweller's shop in his pocket and could at any time command £1000'.

As to the rest she was anything but a bawd but had some reputation for theft, for in the play she becomes almost a female Robin Hood, stealing from the rich to give to the poor. In real life Moll readily admitted to this and also to some forging, but was always adamant that not only had she never been a whore herself but that she would never procure any other woman to become one.

Moll was obviously delighted with her dramatic portrayal and from time to time would sit on a stool on stage to watch the performance. The action of the play concerns the womanising Laxton who seduces women and then blackmails them, a young man who is forbidden to marry the girl of his choice, and 'Jack Dapper' who is trying to avoid being sent to a debtors' prison. During the course of the play characters make various assignations which take place at the Three Pigeons in Brentford. The inn is featured in a number of plays of the period as a refuge for eloping couples or adulterous husbands and wives (and even much later in *She Stoops to Conquer*), the in-joke being that it was owned by a popular actor, Jack Lowin.

All three plots are eventually sorted out by Moll, in the course of which she challenges Laxton, who has taken a fancy to her when dressed as a woman, to a duel. When he agrees he discovers that not only is he hopelessly outclassed but that Moll insists on telling him on behalf of all women exactly what she thinks of him; which suggests that Dekker and Middleton were well aware of her personal views on the subject:

> thou art one of those,
> That thinks each woman thy fond flexible whore:
> If she but casts a liberal eye upon thee,
> Turns back her head, she's thine; or amongst company
> By chance drink first to thee, then she's quite gone.
> There is no means to help her; nay, for a need
> Will swear unto thy credulous fellow lechers
> That thou are more in favour with the lady
> At first sight, than her monkey all her lifetime.
> How many of our sex, by such as thou,
> Have had their good thoughts paid with a blasted name,
> That never deserved so lowly? Or did trip
> In path of whoredom beyond cup and lip,
> But for the stain of conscience and of soul?[3]

The play ends by suggesting the possibility that Moll herself might soon be seen sitting on the stage and might even join the actors to acknowledge applause at the end if the audience wished it:

The Roaring Girl herself, some few days hence,
Shall on this stage give larger recompense,
Which mirth that you may share in, herself doth woo you,
And craves this sign, your hand to beckon her to you.

But there it looks as if she did a great deal more than sit and watch and later actually played herself, for a court indictment dated 12 February 1611–12 states categorically that she had appeared on the stage of the Fortune Theatre some nine months earlier. No explanation is given as to why the case took so long to come to court. What happened next is described in a letter from a John Chamberlain to a friend:

> This Sunday Moll Cutpurse a notorious baggage that was used to go in men's apparel was brought to St. Paul's Cross, where she wept bitterly and seemed very penitent, but it is since doubted this was so but that she was drunk, being discovered to have tippled some three quarts of sack before she came to her penance. She had the daintiest preacher, or ghostly father, that ever I saw in a pulpit, one Ratcliffe of Brazen Nose of Oxford, a likelier man to have led the revels in some Masque at Court than to be where he was, but the best is he did so extremely badly and so wearied his audience that the best part went away and rest tarried to hear Moll Cutpurse rather than himself.

Moll spent the next six months in the notorious Bridewell Prison, beating hemp while being urged to ponder on her sins.

On her release she immediately returned again to the poets and players, almost all of whom she was to outlive. When she was in her fifties, she acted as a spy and courier for the Royalist cause during the Civil War and is authentically reported to have actually robbed General Fairfax on Hounslow Heath, shooting him in the arm and killing the two horses on which his servants were riding. Hotly pursued by soldiers, she was apprehended at Turnham Green and sent to Newgate. But she was to escape the scaffold. Her sheer nerve and spirit so appealed to Fairfax that he allowed her to be ransomed for the enormous sum of £2,000. She died in her small house in Fleet Street on 26 July 1659 at the age of seventy-four and was buried in the churchyard of St Bride's, now the journalists' church, which seems appropriate. In her will she left £20 'so that the conduits might run with wine on the restoration of the King'.

TWELVE

Shakespeare and the King's Men

But this rough magic
I do here abjure; and when I have requir'd
Some heavenly music – which even now I do –
To work mine end upon their senses that
This airy charm is for, I'll break my staff,
Bury it certain fathoms in the earth,
And deeper than did ever plummet sound
I'll drown my book.

Shakespeare, *The Tempest*, V, i

The King's Men were fortunate for even before they acquired their second theatre the fact that they had a royal patron meant that from the start they were able to achieve a certain amount of security in an increasingly cold financial climate. For the plague epidemic of the year of the Queen's death and the accession of James was, if anything, even worse than that of ten years earlier. As the rhyme said:

Whole households and whole streets are stricken,
The sick do die, the sound do sicken.
And Lord have mercy on us crying,
Ere mercy come, that they are dying.

But although the epidemic abated somewhat towards the end of 1604, the disease did not go away and for the next ten years the playhouses were regularly closed for anything from a few weeks to several months, leaving all too many of those involved in the theatre unemployed and struggling to make ends meet. The King's Men had the additional bonus of regularly being commanded to play at Court and in 1606 they had the opportunity not only to earn some money but also to flatter their illustrious patron.

King James had invited the Queen's brother, King Christian IV of Denmark, to England on a state visit. It was to be a grand affair, the entertainment lavish, so it was therefore to be expected that the King's own company of players should perform before the royal guest. The actor Richard Huggett in his book, *The Curse of Macbeth*, suggests that Shakespeare might well have been summoned in person to the office of the comptroller in Whitehall Palace, have had the situation explained to him and be then asked, as a member of the King's own company, to provide a new and suitable play for the occasion. As ever, scholars disagree, but the consensus of the majority of academics is that Shakespeare did indeed write *Macbeth* especially for the event and that it was performed before the Court during the summer of 1606, probably on 7 August, although the first recorded public performance was that seen by Simon Forman at the Globe five years later.

There is much to suggest this is true, since what better subject to please the King than a play featuring two Scottish kings, the spirits of five others and his ancestor, Banquo, while also drawing attention to his expertise in witchcraft? Possibly Shakespeare read the King's own book on the subject, *Daemonologie*, to acquire the mood for it, and he certainly read Holinshed's *Chronicles of Scotland*. He might also have known that when the King visited Oxford the previous year Dr Matthew Gwinn, a Fellow of St John's College, had laid on an entertainment entitled *The Three Sybils* derived from 'three women in strange and wild apparel . . . either the Weird Sisters, that is (as ye would say) the goddesses of destiny or else some nymphs or fairies who accost Macbeth and Banquo'. If that is so then it could well have been why Forman described the three witches in *Macbeth* as looking like nymphs or fairies rather than the wizened old women of popular mythology. Another suggestion is that the play is as short as it is because it was designed to suit the King's attention span; it was not unusual for him to go to sleep during theatrical performances.

161

Although *Macbeth* remains to this day one of Shakespeare's most popular plays and still packs in audiences, it has carried an enormous amount of baggage with it over the last four hundred years. Popular legend has it that it almost inevitably brings bad luck with it, that a production can lead to death, doom and disaster for all those involved. In his book Huggett writes that the famous 'curse of Macbeth' struck at the very first performance when Hal Berridge, the boy playing Lady Macbeth, was taken ill and that Shakespeare himself was forced to take over the role.[1] He claims John Aubrey as the source but this writer has so far been unable to track down the reference. But even if it could be found it should perhaps be greeted with caution in view of other theatrical information peddled by Aubrey for according to him Ben Jonson 'killed Mr. Marlowe, the Poet, on Bunhill, comeing [*sic*] from the Greencurtain playhouse'.[2] Some claim that the 'curse' is in the text of the play itself because the famous chant given to the witches which begins 'Fillet of a fenny's snake, Eye of newt and toe of frog . . .' is an authentic black magic spell. It is also suggested that so far from pleasing the King the emphasis on witchcraft and the way it was dealt with upset him, which is why no other performance was recorded for five years, but if this was the case, then there is no record of it.

Given the financially hard times those dramatists were fortunate that had other ways of earning an income. It seems that few of them by then were also actors, as had sometimes been the case in the past. We do not know when Shakespeare gave up acting or how good he was, although he was obviously sufficiently competent to remain a member of the acting company for a number of years. Apart from the role of Master Knowell in Jonson's *Every Man In His Humour*, there is only hearsay evidence as to parts he played. His brother Gilbert, now established as a haberdasher, did visit London to see his brother's plays and watch him act (possibly Edmund too), and is said to have told a neighbour on his return to Stratford that he had seen Will play Adam in *As You Like It* and that he was 'brought on to the stage on another man's back', presumably that of the actor playing Orlando.[3] Theatre tradition also gives him the ghost in *Hamlet* and the far more showy, and unlikely roles of Mercutio in

Romeo and Juliet and Berowne in *Love's Labour's Lost*, though the actor Ian Richardson, who played Berowne for the Royal Shakespeare Company, became convinced that he was playing 'the man himself. I know that there is some scholarly dispute about that but I think Dr. Rowse would agree. Here is Shakespeare talking, here he is with all his verbal quips . . . it is the only Shakespeare role I have played where, on the last performance, I wept.'[4] If he did continue well into the early 1600s then it must have been by choice.

George Chapman who, as we know, had financial problems right from the start, supplemented his income with translation, tackling first Homer's *Iliad* and then the *Odyssey*, under the patronage of the King's eldest son, Prince Henry, on the understanding that once he had completed the first part of the task he would have a pension for life. The *Iliad* was finally published in 1611 and he must have sighed with relief as he saw security finally within his grasp, but unfortunately Prince Henry died that same year and the King reneged on the arrangement, leaving Chapman to face his most serious financial crisis yet and a great deal of debt.

The profession widely regarded as having a licence to print money is that of the law, and three of the Jacobean dramatists, John Marston, John Ford and John Webster all trained as lawyers, when it might well be that they also developed a taste for theatre since plays were a popular form of entertainment at the Middle Temple, where they all studied. Marston's father, a Shropshire lawyer, was the Recorder of Coventry when Marston was born and became Lent Reader at the Middle Temple in 1592. On 2 August of that year the sixteen-year-old Marston was 'especially' admitted to the Middle Temple by his father. He was a very privileged student and a bright future had beckoned him, as two years later he achieved his first degree. But he had started writing for publication almost as soon as he began to study.

'Eroticism and satire', writes M.C. Bradbrook in her biography of John Webster, 'both fashionable, were Marston's scandalous choice for poetry of an ambivalent, yet pointed, wit.' He soon involved himself in the world of the playhouses, although records suggest that from time to time he returned to the Middle Temple and undertook some legal work, probably sharing his father's chambers there until, in 1599, his father died, leaving his own law books 'to him whom I hoped would have profited by them in the study of the law, but man proposeth and God disposeth'.[5]

Thereafter for some years it seems God disposed that Marston would devote his time to his theatrical interests, rather than his official profession. At least his father did not live to see the part played by his son in the well-publicised Poets' War or the trouble he was in over *Eastward Ho!* Marston had his greatest success in 1604 with his play *The Malcontent*, but after that he started to lose his taste for it and some time in 1607 began to study seriously for the ministry. The next time we hear of him, on 8 June 1608, he has been committed to Newgate gaol on an unspecified charge, although it is thought that this was a formality to do with some kind of a legal infringement connected with the breaking up of the Queen's Revels Company in which he then had a share, not anything political or serious. On 24 September 1609 he was made a Deacon in the Parish Church of Stanton Harcourt, went from there to St Mary's Hall, Oxford, to study further and on 18 June 1610 was ordained priest before finally, some years later, being given the lucrative living of Christchurch in Hampshire. He had come a long way from the precocious law student who first made his name with *Metamorphosis of Pygmalion's Image*, described by Bradbrook as 'frankly pornographic'.

Of the second of the trio of lawyers, John Ford, we know very little except that he spent his entire adult life hard up and casting round for funds. Born in 1586 into a family of Devon gentry, he was related to the then Lord Chief Justice Popham. After possibly studying at Exeter College, Oxford, he was admitted to the Middle Temple where his behaviour was sufficiently bad for him to be sent down for two years. His misdemeanours included taking part in a protest against 'wearing caps in hall' and not paying his bills. His first published work appeared in 1606 but his early plays are among those lost by Warburton's cook and he remains best known for his extraordinary *'Tis Pity She's a Whore*, which is actually about incest not prostitution, and various collaborations with Dekker.

His father died in 1610, presumably having given up on him, his will having been drawn up by John's brother, Henry, wherein it was willed: 'To John Ford, gent, my brother twenty pounds a year for the term of his life . . . upon condition he surrender the estate he hath of two tenements called Glandfields grounds in Bilver park and willow meade, lying in Ipplepen and Torbryam, to the use of my children.' This at least gave him a small but regular income and it does seem that from time to time he returned to the law to earn a meagre income. An odd description of him survives in two lines of anonymous verse:

> Deep in a dump John Ford was got
> With folded arms and melancholy hat.

However out of the three lawyers it is John Webster, whom we first came across in 1602 writing for Henslowe, who managed successfully to combine working in the theatre with both law and the family business. T.S. Eliot's verse about him is well known:

> Webster was much possessed by death,
> And saw the skull beneath the skin
> And breastless creatures underground
> Leaned backward with a lipless grin.

An unkind description of him, penned by a Henry Fitzjeffrey, claims:

> But h'st! with him Crabbed Websterio,
> The playwright, cartwright: whether? either? ho?
> No further, look as ye'd be looked into:
> Sit as he would read: Lord, who knows of him?
> Was ever man so mangled with a poem?
> See how he draws his mouth awry of late,
> How he scrubs; wrings his wrists; scratches his pate.
> A midwife! Help! By his Brain's coitus,
> Some centaur strange: some huge Bucephalus,
> Or Pallas (sure) engendered in his brain,
> Strike Vulcan with thy hammer once again.[6]

It is particularly insulting and snobbish as it describes him as 'a cartwright' much in the way the University Wits, and Henslowe when angry, referred to Ben Jonson as a 'a bricklayer'. Although, as a writer Webster is associated with dark deeds and violent death because of his two great plays, *The Duchess of Malfi* and *The White Devil*, there is nothing to suggest that he was a particularly depressed or gloomy person. He had been born into a comfortable household, his father being a successful coachbuilder (hence 'cartwright') and probably went to the Merchant Taylors School before being admitted to the Middle Temple to study law. The small body of work that has come down to us does suggest that he might well have had a reputation for writing slowly and with some difficulty, and it is unlikely that he could ever have made a good living only from plays, but then he did not need to for once he had qualified it seems he took over the legal and administrative side of the family firm, leaving his father and brother to see to its practical side.

The White Devil, the first of the two famous tragedies both based on real events, was first performed during the winter of 1611–12 at the Red Bull theatre, Webster choosing that particular playhouse because he rated the company's young leading actor, Richard Perkins, very highly indeed. He actually mentions him in the published postcript to the play: 'In particular I must remember the well-approved industry of my friend, Master Perkins, and confess the worth of his action from beginning to end.' This was the first time any actor had been so honoured, including Alleyn or Burbage. But, Perkins apart, it was not a particularly good choice of venue for the Red Bull has been described as 'a rowdy house with a vulgar audience', although in fact it was more what we would describe today as a neighbourhood theatre, providing popular fare for local people. It also presented all kinds of spectacles, such as firework displays and pageants, supplementing its income by hiring out costumes and properties.

Unsurprisingly therefore, given the play's complexities, it was not a success. 'Ignorant asses' is how Webster described his audience at its first performance. M.C. Bradbrook suggests that at least he could console himself with the thought that in the previous year Ben Jonson's second attempt at Senecan tragedy, *Catiline*, had fallen just as flat as his *Sejanus* had some years earlier. Possibly it was *The White Devil* that prompted Fitzjeffrey's catty poem for he finished it:

> But what care I, it [the play] will be so obscure
> That none shall understand him I am sure.

The reception he received for *The Duchess of Malfi*, however, a year or so later was very different, not least because this time his play was performed by the King's Men in the Blackfriars Theatre and to a far more sophisticated audience. It was chosen for production by John Hemings, and when Webster published the script he named the leading actors along with the parts that they played. John Lowin, now recognised as a leading actor, played Bosola; Burbage, the Duchess's murderous brother, Ferdinand, Duke of Calabria; Henry Condell, the evil Cardinal of Aragon, and young Richard Sharpe, the Duchess. The part of Antonio, the Duchess's steward who becomes her second husband, was played by William Osler, who died not long after its first production. The play proved popular right from the start, not only because it was put on in the right place to the right people, but because the story is a great deal less complicated and more accessible than that of the *White Devil* and its tragic heroine is so sympathetic. Crowds flocked to see it and as late as 1635 it was chosen for a command performance before King Charles and his Court.

During the winter of 1614–15 Webster's father died, leaving his two sons a considerable estate. Edward Webster renewed the lease on the family property in February 1615 and John took out his 'freedom by patrimony' of the Merchant Taylors as he was now sufficiently well off to be able to afford his 'Freedom of the City', which enabled him to vote in the Common Council and enjoy coveted trading privileges. He wrote little for the theatre after this but did become involved in writing and putting on city pageants.

The decade from 1603 to 1613 was to see some of the very finest Jacobean plays. From Shakespeare, after *Macbeth*, *Antony and*

Cleopatra, Coriolanus, The Winter's Tale and *The Tempest* were still to come along with the lesser *Timon of Athens, Pericles* and *Cymbeline,* and it is now generally agreed that he collaborated with John Fletcher on *Henry VIII* and *The Two Noble Kinsmen.* Ben Jonson's great *Volpone* also had its first production in 1606 and was followed later by *The Alchemist,* not to mention the work of Middleton, Dekker, Webster, Beaumont and Fletcher and the rest. But over and above it all, especially towards the end of that period, there is a sense of fragmentation, that the theatrical world as it had been known was beginning to break up.

On 3 July 1613 Sir Henry Wotton sat down and wrote a letter to his nephew, Sir Edmund Bacon, informing him of a dramatic event which had taken place four days earlier on 29 June:

> Now to let matters of State sleep, I will entertain you at present with what hath happened this week at the Bank's side. The King's Players had a new play called *All is True,* representing the principle [*sic*] pieces of the reign of Henry VIII which was set forth with many extraordinary circumstances of pomp and majesty, even to the matting of the stage; the Knights of the Order with their Georges and Garters, the Guards with their embroidered coats, and the like: sufficient in truth, within a while, to make greatness very familiar if not ridiculous.
>
> Now King Henry, making a masque at Cardinal Wolsey's house, and certain chambers [cannon] being shot off at his entry, some of the paper, or other stuff wherewith one of them was stuffed, did light on the thatch, where being thought at first but an idle smoke, and their eyes more attentive to the show, it kindled inwardly, and ran round like a train [of gunpowder], consuming within less than an hour the whole house to the very grounds. This was the fatal period of that virtuous fabric, wherein nothing did perish but wood and straw, and a few forsaken cloaks; only one man had his breeches set on fire, that would perhaps have broiled him if he had not by the benefit of provident wit, put it out with bottle ale.[7]

Burbage must have thanked Providence that he had acquired the Blackfriars since he was now able to transfer his entire operation over the river. The sharers immediately made plans for a new theatre. The new and improved Globe rose from the ashes of the old within a year, at a cost of £1,400, and was described by John Chamberlain in a letter dated 30 June 1614 as 'the fairest that ever was in England'.

It was also that same year that Shakespeare made his last major property purchase, a smart house in Blackfriars, which seems somewhat strange as he was now spending more and more time in Stratford to the point where John Fletcher had virtually taken over from him as resident dramatist of the King's Men. The Blackfriars property, a large dwelling, was conveyed to him on 10 March of that year at a cost of £140, of which he put £80 down as a deposit, the balance of £60 to be paid off as a mortgage. The Conveyance Deed according to the relevant documents tell us that the 'dwelling house, shops, cellars, sollars, plot of ground and singular other the premises above, by the presents mentioned, to be bargained and sold and every part and parcel thereof with the appurtenances, unto the said William Shakespeare and William Johnson, John Jackson and John Hemmings'.[8]

The three men were his sureties for his mortgage. Hemings, as we know, was his friend and fellow sharer in the King's Men, Jackson was a city merchant and Johnson the landlord of the actors' favourite tavern, the Mermaid. They were never called on to honour their guarantees for Shakespeare paid off his mortgage in full and on time. He then created a trusteeship for his London property which, on his death, was to be sold off on behalf of his family with the profits going to them. A very different picture, this, from the position in which the hard-working and prolific Thomas Dekker found himself and who, at the same time, was arrested for debt and spent the next three years in and out of debtors' prisons.

Yet another sign of the passing of an era was the death, two years later, of Robert Armin, the last of the great clowns for whom Shakespeare had specifically written. At this point Ben Jonson, who must have had some realisation of what was happening and who alone among his contemporaries saw his work as something for posterity, collected together his best poetry and existing play texts and in 1616 had them published in a Folio edition. King James, recognising his status as poet and dramatist, awarded him a pension for life. The year 1616 also saw the death of Francis Beaumont. Whatever his relationship with Fletcher might have been, three years earlier he had married Ursula, heiress to Henry Sly of Sundridge in Kent. There were two daughters of the marriage, the younger, Frances, born posthumously. Beaumont died on 6 March 1616, the cause unknown, but he achieved burial in Westminster Abbey.

His death, however, was totally overshadowed by that of another, for on 23 April, Shakespeare died at his home in Stratford. His father had died in 1601, his mother in 1608, both having reached a decent age, but their children, with the exception of their daughter Joan, were not long-lived. Gilbert had died in 1612 at the age of forty-five and Richard the following year at the age of thirty-nine. Death was also taking its toll elsewhere. Shakespeare had named his twins Hamnet and Judith after his friends the Sadlers, and in 1614 Judith Sadler died as did another old friend, John Combe, who is buried next to Shakespeare in Holy Trinity Church.

It is ironic that Shakespeare, who had so successfully avoided scandal while living in a hotbed of it in London, was to find himself embroiled in a local one only weeks before his death. On 10 February 1616 Judith Shakespeare, now aged thirty-one and considered an elderly spinster, finally married Thomas Quiney. The couple were married at Holy Trinity Church but were then immediately summoned to appear before the consistory court in Worcester for marrying without a proper licence. Quiney refused to attend and was promptly excommunicated; no mention is made as to whether or not Judith suffered the same fate. The problem arose because a special licence was needed for Lent weddings and although the banns had been properly called for three weeks, no such licence had been applied for. But worse was to come.

There is a possible reason for such sudden haste to the wedding. While supposedly courting Judith in what can only be described as a leisurely fashion, Thomas had been involved in an affair with a young woman called Margaret Wheeler who was now having his child. The proper and expected thing for him to do was to marry her, not Judith. But he chose not to, possibly because he was aware of the advantages of marrying into a well-off family, and marriage to Judith would release him from this obligation. Poor Margaret, after suffering a difficult pregnancy, died in childbirth along with her baby a month after the marriage. They were buried on 15 March.

This time Quiney was summonsed before an ecclesiastical court especially set up to deal with cases of 'whoredom and uncleanness' (popularly known as 'bawdy courts'), and he appeared before it on 26 March confessing to having had *carnalem copulacionem*, carnal copulation, with 'the said Wheeler' and was sentenced to the usual punishment for such an offence: to perform open penance, dressed in a white sheet, before the church congregation for three Sundays in a row. Unusually, and possibly due to his father-in-law's influence, this was commuted to paying a fine to the parish and acknowledging his crime, fully dressed, before the minister of Bishopton Chapel. Not surprisingly a marriage off to such a poor start was doomed from the outset.

In January, Shakespeare had called in his friend, the lawyer Francis Collins, and drafted his will, which was substantially altered in March, possibly as a result of Judith's marriage, signing that he was at that time 'in perfect health and memory'. A host of causes, all surmise, have been suggested as the cause of his death: that he died, variously, of alcoholism, Bright's disease, exposure after sleeping a night under a crab-apple tree (!), typhus, cholera, paralysis, epilepsy, apoplexy, arterio-sclerosis, excessive smoking, angina pectoris, pulmonary congestion and syphilis. The best-known one, which has something of the ring of truth, is that put forward by a later vicar of Stratford, the Revd John Ward, in 1662 and might well have still been extant locally. 'Shakespeare, Drayton and Ben Jonson had a merry meeting and it seemed drank too hard for Shakespeare died of a fever there contracted.'[9]

It is quite possible to believe that the three met up in Warwickshire that spring; indeed the Bell Inn at Welford just outside Stratford claims to be the meeting place. Drayton, now an established poet, lived in Nuneaton, an easy day's ride away, while Jonson took any opportunity to call on friends out of town. To this day local tradition has Shakespeare either walking back home along the path beside the Avon, which still exists, or riding back on horseback along the Evesham road. Either way he is said to have become thoroughly soaked. If this was the case and if, as was probable, he had retired to Stratford exhausted and drained from his vast output of work, then he might indeed have died of 'pulmonary congestion', in other words, pneumonia.

The Burial register reads: '1616 April 25. Will Shakespeare, gent.' His position in the town entitled him to be buried inside the church within the chancel rail and it is for his standing in the local community, not his reputation as a playwright and poet, that he lies where he does. He is said to have been buried seventeen feet down but this is hardly possible so close to the River Avon. He is also credited with writing his own epitaph:

> Good frend for Jesus sake forbeare,
> To dig the duste encloased here;
> ET
> Blest Be Y Man YU spares thes stones
> And curst be he Y moves my bones.

An entire industry has grown up around his epitaph alone and constant requests have been made to open up the grave in the hope that by so doing his authorship might in some way be 'proved'. But those who still prefer to believe that Shakespeare did not write Shakespeare have never been able to explain how he was able to fool the actors among whom he worked for the best part of a quarter of a century, during which time he also lived among and mixed with all the other playwrights of the day from Marlowe through Jonson to Middleton and Fletcher. Or why, in his will, he left to 'my fellows' John Hemings, Henry Condell and Richard Burbage 'a peece [that is money] to buy them rings'. Not to mention Ben Jonson's poetic tribute to him as 'Soul of our age!, the applause! the wonder of our stage!', telling how he outshone Lily, 'sporting

Kyd and Marlowe's mighty line'. That he will stay alive so long as his works live:

> Shine forth, thou Star of Poets, and with rage
> Or influence, chide or cheer the drooping stage.

Prospero had finally left his magic island, abjured his 'rough magic', broken his staff, drowned his books and set the creatures of his imagination free. He had nothing more to say.

THIRTEEN

An Insult to Spain

The Poet's eye, in a fine frenzy rolling,
Doth glance from heaven to earth, from earth to heaven,
And as imagination bodies forth
The forms of things unknown; the Poet's pen
Turns them to shapes, and gives to airy nothing,
A local habitation, and a name.
Such tricks hath strong imagination.

Shakespeare, A Midsummer Night's Dream, V, i

In the March of 1618 another major theatrical light went out with the death of Richard Burbage. He had risen with Edward Alleyn in the late 1580s, matched him for ten years, then, as Alleyn gradually withdrew from the stage at the end of the century, had gone on to become the greatest actor of his day, unrivalled over a span of twenty years. He had not only done his writers proud, he was both respected and much loved within his profession and in an age of gossip and the hothouse atmosphere of that profession it is impossible to find anyone who had a bad word to say of him.

Those who saw him act vied with each other afterwards to describe the effect he had on audiences. There are several versions of the *Funeral Elegy on the death of the famous Actor Richard Burbage: who died Saturday in Lent, the 13 March 1618*:

The Play now ended, think his grave to be
The retiring house of his sad Tragedie,
Where to give his fame this, be not afraid
Here lies the best Tragedian ever played.
No more young Hamlet though but scant of breath

Shall cry revenge for his dear father's death:
Poor Romeo never more shall tears beget
For Juliet's love and cruel Capulet:
Harry shall not be seen as King or Prince,
They died with thee, dear Dick
Not to revive again. Jeronimo
Shall cease to mourn his son, Horatio,
Edward shall lack a representative,
And Crookback, as befits, shall cease to live.
Tyrant Macbeth with unwash'd bloody hand,
We vainly now may hope to understand.
Brutus and Marcus henceforth must be dumb
For ne'er their like upon our stage shall come
To charm the faculty of eyes and ears,
Unless we could command the dead to rise . . .
Heartbroke Philaster and Amintas too
Are left forever with the red-haired Jew,
Which sought the bankrupt merchant's pound of flesh
By woman lawyer caught in his own mesh.

The list of characters referred to in the Elegie, of which this is
only a part, shows that, as well as his roles in Shakespeare's plays in
his own day, Burbage was equally famed for his performances in
those of Kyd, Marlowe, Jonson, Beaumont and Fletcher, and other
contemporary dramatists.

Richard Corbet wrote of how, by his brilliance, he could 'change
with ease from Ancient Lear to youthful Pericles':

What a wide world, the Globe thy fittest place!
Thy stature small, but every thought and mood
Might thoroughly from thy face be understood.

After listing various roles Burbage had made his own he concludes:

Thereafter must our poets leave to write,
Since thou art gone, dear Dick, a tragic night

Will wrap our black-hung stage. He made a Poet.
And those who yet remain full surely know it.
For having Burbage to give forth each line
It filled the brain with fury more divine.[1]

But renowned as he might have been as Jonson's 'subtle Alchemist' and Volpone or Kyd's Hieronimo in *Spanish Tragedy*, it is his creation of Shakespeare's roles that still overshadows them all. He is first remembered as a young actor playing one of the Antipholus twins in *Comedy of Errors*, followed by Petruchio, Romeo, and Benedict. Thomas Nashe wrote of him that when he played the chivalrous Talbot in the *Henry VI* plays, it had seemed to him during the time he was in the theatre that England's great military hero actually 'lived again'. 'Crookback' Richard III also came early but it was a role Burbage would play for the rest of his life so convincingly that 'a simple innkeeper mistook a player for a King', not least when he cried real tears on Bosworth Field. There were so many more, Richard II with his splendid poetry, Prince Hal growing into Henry V, Shylock 'in a red wig', 'the grieved Moor' Othello, and 'ancient Lear'. Tradition has it that in common with a number of serious actors today he also played Malvolio. Prospero is not listed in the many contemporary tributes but it is hard to imagine that he did not also play that last great role.

No actor since has ever had written for him such a range of parts. Writer and player found each other at exactly the right point in time. 'He made a Poet', wrote Corbet. Shakespeare was indeed magnificently served by his great friend and colleague, but 'made a Poet'? If this is true, then it might also be said that the Poet made the Actor.

It was during that same summer that Ben Jonson was to pay his famous, or notorious, visit to Sir William Drummond at his Scottish home, Hawthornden Castle.[2] Jonson walked the whole way from London, presumably from choice since he was well able to afford the hire of a horse. Dekker describes Jonson's appearance at this time as 'having a face like a bruised, rotten russet-apple, or a badly pock-marked warming pan'. As he stomped steadily north he had plenty of time to consider both his past life and his present situation. He no longer fought duels nor would he again risk prison for the sake of a good joke; his wilder years now lay behind him. He had suffered loss, first his baby daughter then, in 1601, his eldest son had died of the plague as the result of which, he was to tell Drummond, he suffered a strange experience. At the time of the boy's death he was staying in the country with Sir Robert Cotton, when he suddenly awoke in the middle of the night to see a vision of the boy 'with a mark of a bloody cross on his forehead as if he had been cut with a sword'. Thoroughly shaken, the next morning Jonson told his host of his nightmare. Cotton's response was to reassure him that it was 'but an apprehension of his fantasy' and to take no notice of it, but shortly afterwards Jonson received a message from his wife, Anne, telling him that the boy was indeed dead. All that was left was for Jonson to write his epitaph:

> Rest in soft peace and asked, say here doth lie
> Ben Jonson, his best piece of poetry.

There had been no more children and the Jonsons had drifted apart. As he told Drummond later, he had not 'bedded' Anne for five years.

With regard to his work his plays, particularly *Volpone*, *The Alchemist* and *Bartholomew Fair*, remained popular and he had also had considerable success with the more recent *The Devil's an Ass*, performed by the King's Men. The story is that of an apprentice demon who feels he is being given tasks far beneath his ability and so persuades Satan, much against the latter's better judgement, to send him up to earth to corrupt the City of London. Arriving in the heart of the City, he assiduously sets about trying to corrupt the merchants, bankers and city fathers only to find he is completely outclassed. Finally, unable to cope, he has to beg Satan to rescue him, promising that he will make ropes out of sand and catch the wind in a net, rather than 'stay me here a thought more'. Whereupon an infuriated Satan arrives in a clap of thunder to take his failed demon back to Hell. Since financial malpractice, corruption and conmen are still with us, it is not surprising that a recent production of the play by the Royal Shakespeare Company was a great success.

But Jonson was becoming increasingly disillusioned with the theatre due to the the popular passion for elaborate masques. While he was prepared to write these, since he was well paid for doing so, he felt as many writers do today that his work was being swamped by what we would call designers' theatre. Paired most often with the most famous stage designer of the day, Inigo Jones, he was finding that his words were now secondary to exotic sets and magnificent costumes, leading him to confide to Prince Charles that 'when he wanted a word to express the greatest villain in the world, he called him "an Inigo"'.

When he arrived in Scotland his first port of call was Edinburgh, where he received a civic reception in recognition of the publication of his works two years earlier, even though there were those back home who had accused him of arrogance for so doing. It was also to acknowledge that he was about to receive an honorary degree from the University of Oxford. While in the city he was caught up with none other than John Taylor, 'the water poet', he who had been howled off the stage of the Hope Theatre for failing to entertain a rowdy audience with a supposed insult competition and his poetry. He, too, had walked the whole way but through necessity rather than choice and by the time he reached Edinburgh he was in a sorry state. His must have been the first sponsored walk for before setting out he had persuaded a number of people to pay sums of money to him on his return if he successfully completed the round trip. He must have been in a bad way, for Jonson felt sufficiently sorry for him to help him out financially.

He then went on to Hawthornden. Presumably Drummond had actually invited him to stay but he could hardly have known what he would be in for. Soon Jonson was nightly regaling his host and his friends with London Court scandal and theatrical gossip. As he began drinking his way steadily through Drummond's cellar he also moved on to his favourite subject: himself. How when young he was 'much given to venery', that he thought 'going to bed with a maid nothing to the enjoyment of the wantonness of a wife' (someone else's wife, that is), and that while married he had lain with another woman diverse times who allowed him all privileges 'except that last act that she would not agree to'. Quite possibly many women did not allow full sexual intercourse with their lovers; Elizabethan or Jacobean woman of childbearing age and normal fertility were playing Russian roulette every time they made love.

Whether Drummond, who seems to have been a quiet and studious kind of person, appreciated such confidences he does not say. He made a note of Jonson's opinions of other writers, such as 'that Chapman's translations of Homer and Virgil . . . were but prose; that Donne, for not keeping of the accent [beat] deserved hanging; that Sharpham, Day and Dekker were all rogues . . .'. That 'Drayton feared him', 'Francis Beaumont loved too much himself and his own verses' (a case of the pot calling the kettle black), 'that he once beat Marston and took his pistol from him' and that Marston 'wrote his father-in-law's preachings and his father-in-law his [Marston's] comedies'. That the boy actor, Nathan Field, was 'his scholar', and that 'Markham was a plagiarist and a base fellow like Thomas Middleton'. Also that Shakespeare, in a play, had 'brought in a number of men saying they had suffered shipwreck in Bohemia, where there is no sea nearer than some hundred miles'.

As for the Court, Queen Elizabeth 'never saw herself in the mirror after she became old', Leicester's wife, affirmed Jonson, 'poisoned him with a potion given to her to cure faintness', while Sir Philip Sidney had been 'no pleasant man in countenance, his face being spoiled with pimples'. He claimed close friendship with Sir Walter Ralegh, who had been foolish enough to have sufficient faith in him to send him to France with his own son to keep an eye on the lad. Jonson blamed his own subsequent activities, concerning 'damsels' and getting drunk, on the proclivities of young Ralegh who, from time to time, had to haul his mentor back to their lodgings 'on a cart'. He also confided in Drummond that during his time in prison after killing Gabriel Spenser, he had for a short time become a Catholic convert, a recusant, 'and that at his first communion, in true token of reconciliation, he had drunk out all the full cup of wine'. After the way he was getting through his host's wine, Drummond was hardly surprised to learn that on occasion, after a heavy evening's drinking, 'he [Jonson] hath consumed a whole night in lying looking to his great toe, about which he has seen Tartars and Turks, Romans and Carthaginians fight in his imagination'.

Finally, to Drummond's great relief, Jonson at last set off back home to London, leaving his host to contemplate a cellar full of empty bottles. 'He is', wrote Drummond,

> a great lover and praiser of himself, a contemner and scorner of others, given rather to lose a friend than a jest, jealous of every word and action of those about him (especially after a drink which is one of the elements in which he liveth), a dissembler of ill parts which reign in him, a bragger of some good that he wanteth, thinketh nothing well but what either he himself or some of his friends and countrymen hath said and done. He is passionately kind and angry, careless either to gain or keep, vindictive but if he be well answered, at himself. Interpreteth best saying and deeds often to the worst, oppressed with fantasy, which hath ever mastered his reason: a general disease in many poets.[3]

Either unaware or uncaring of the reputation he had left behind, on 10 May 1619 Jonson wrote to Drummond asking if he would undertake a little research for him on a project on which he was engaged, sending along with his good wishes to Drummond his regards to a formidable list of people he had met while staying with him. There is no record of Drummond's reply but he deserves a vote of thanks for recording Jonson's stay in such detail and also how the fame of the London dramatists had spread far enough north for people to want to hear about them at first hand.

The golden age of the playwrights was now rapidly drawing to its end although the early 1620s still produced some interesting work, one example being a play rushed on to the stage while the events on which it was based were still a talking point. *The Witch of Edmonton* was a joint collaboration by Thomas Dekker, John Ford and William Rowley. Rowley, a contemporary of Ford, wrote almost entirely in collaboration with other people. In 1609, after making little headway as a dramatist in his own right and somewhat against the trend, he became an actor with the Duke of York's (late Prince Charles's) Men mainly playing comedy parts. He would, however, continue to collaborate on scripts, not least with Middleton on *The Changeling*.

The Witch of Edmonton was given its first performance not long after the supposed witch, who gives the play its title, was hanged for witchcraft at Tyburn on 16 April 1621. On 27 April, only eleven days later, a pamphlet was published, *The Wonderful Discovery of Elizabeth Sawyer, Witch, Late of Edmonton*, written by 'Henry Goodcole, Minister of the Word of God, and her continual visitor in the Gaol of Newgate', in which he detailed her supposed witchcraft and the crimes she was alleged to have committed, a copy of which must have been picked up by one or other of the writers. Given the eerie thrill such a subject was likely to give an audience, it must have seemed to them that a play based around such an immediately topical instance of witchcraft was likely to be a real crowd-puller. For there is no doubt that most of the population shared the views of King James, believed in witches and would continue to do so for some considerable time. Twenty years later Witchfinder General Matthew Hopkins was to oversee the hanging of sixty women in Essex who had been accused of witchcraft.

In a period when any eccentric old woman, especially if she was unfortunate enough to have some physical deformity, could all too easily be made a scapegoat for all local ills, Elizabeth Sawyer fitted the picture only too well as by all accounts she was an unprepossessing-looking woman with only one eye. During her interrogation she was asked how she had suffered this loss, to which she replied: 'With a stick which one of my children had in hand; that night my mother did die it was done, for I was stooping by the bedside and by chance did hit my eye on the sharp end of the stick.' The means by which she was made to 'confess' to witchcraft hardly bear thinking about but during the inquisition she told her torturers that the Devil had appeared to her in the shape of a dog, sometimes black, sometimes white, and that he had 'sucked' her blood from a special teat which she had for that purpose. He had asked for her 'body and soul', or he would tear her to pieces, and when she agreed taught her a three-word Latin spell. She had finally been brought to the attention of the authorities by a local JP, Arthur Robinson, who had carried out a 'test' to 'prove' she was a witch. The test consisted of setting fire to some thatch from her roof while she was out and if this brought her running back, then it would prove her guilt. Needless to say, seeing the smoke, she did run back home and on such flimsy 'evidence', followed by interrogation, she was convicted.

Several different storylines converge at the end of the play but Dekker is credited with that of Elizabeth Sawyer, whom he treats in his version of events with considerable sympathy. From the first we are shown how she is continually persecuted by the people around her to the point where she finally decides that if, in spite of everything she can do or say, she is still regarded as a witch then she might as well claim to be one and see if there is anything to be gained from it since she is continually being blamed for cattle falling sick or crops being blighted. But then matters became far more serious.

'Sir Arthur Clarington', an unflattering and thinly disguised portrait of Arthur Robinson JP, has palmed his pregnant mistress off on an unsuspecting young man (with whom she has also slept) who, since he loves her, agrees to marry her, believing the child to be his. But when he goes home to tell his family that he now has a wife, before he can do so he is more or less ordered by his father to marry a local heiress to save them from ruin. Unable to tell his parents the truth, he duly goes through with the second, and bigamous, wedding. When the first wife turns up and is about to discover what has happened, he decides his only recourse is to murder one of them. Then, when his infamy is discovered, he successfully blames it on having been bewitched by Mother Sawyer. Dekker gives Mother Sawyer knowledge of 'Clarington's' prior involvement with the first bride, along with other of his unsavoury secrets, thus making it imperative he rid himself of her. He even shows him doing the 'thatch test' to which Arthur Robinson testified in court. The play proved to be a hit. Just how closely Sir Arthur Clarington really did resemble Arthur Robinson JP it is impossible to know. One wonders if he saw it and, if so, whether he either did not recognise himself or thought it best to keep his head down.

Two years later, in 1623, Shakespeare's old friends and colleagues John Hemings and Henry Condell published thirty-six of his plays in what is now known as the *First Folio*. Sixteen of them had been previously published in his lifetime in 'Quarto' editions, but it is not known if he had any hand in their publication or supervised how they were printed. His friends put them together, they said, 'in order to keep the memory of so worthy a friend and fellow alive'. A thirty-seventh play, *Pericles*, was added later. Hemings and Condell authenticated the thirty-six plays but presumably had doubts about *Pericles* and *The Two Noble Kinsmen*, which is now credited to Shakespeare and Fletcher.

One last play is worthy of note because it not only caused an almighty furore but almost provoked a war with Spain. In 1624 *A Game At Chess*, performed by the King's Men at the Globe, ran for an unprecedented nine consecutive performances, the first ever long run, grossing the enormous sum of £1,500 at the box office. It also provoked some of the earliest recorded London traffic jams, playgoers blocking the streets in carriages and on foot in their desperation to reach the theatre and find a seat. It also made its author, Thomas Middleton, a wanted man. Hitherto he had kept out of trouble and had recently had considerable success with two very fine plays, *Women Beware Women* and, in collaboration with Rowley, *The Changeling*.

A Game at Chess is a political allegory about the then rapidly deteriorating relations between England and Spain, its meaning crystal clear to the audiences whose popular opinion it represented. The literary sources of the play were taken from a variety of anti-Catholic, anti-Spanish pamphlets, their content repeated almost verbatim, coupled with unambiguous references to the recent mad venture to Spain undertaken by Prince Charles and his friend the Duke of Buckingham, with the object of bringing back with them a royal Spanish bride; an attempt which failed disastrously. In the play the protagonists are symbolised as chess pieces. The white of course are the English and the White King, James I. The black, from the thinly disguised country of 'Gondomar', are the Spanish and the Black King, Philip IV of Spain. During the course of the action the Spanish monarchy and its ambassador are held up to ridicule, the Roman Catholic church is savagely satirised, and in the final scene the whole Spanish nation is consigned to hell.

No wonder it was popular, for it rode on the crest of the wave of anti-Spanish jingoism which was sweeping the country after some 6,000 troops had been sent to Flanders. The King and his Court were out of London for the summer but news of the smash hit, the enormous crowds, and the jammed streets, soon travelled. Towards the end of the first week in August, a John Chamberlain wrote to a friend: 'I doubt not but you have heard of our famous play of Gondomar by all sorts of people – young and old . . . Lady Smith would persuade me to take her to see it but I could not sit so long for we must have been there before one o'clock at farthest to find room.' It must have seemed to the King's Men that the show would run and run.

It was then that the Spanish Ambassador, Don Carlos Coloma, received wind of it and promptly went to see the show himself, emerging absolutely incandescent with rage. 'There were more than three thousand persons there on the day the audience was *smallest!*', he ranted, adding 'that there was so much merriment, hub-bub and applause that had I been many leagues away it would not have been possible for me not to take notice of it'. It was, he continued, 'a very scandalous comedy and acted publicly by the King's own players'.[4] Worst of all his *amour propre* had been insulted, for he had actually been portrayed on stage in person and to ensure that no one was in any doubt as to who was being represented it is said that the players had managed to obtain one of his own cast-off suits for the actor playing the role.

Coloma formally complained to King James in person on behalf of the Spanish government, threatening drastic action. Faced with the possibility of a complete breakdown in relations between Spain and England, James was appalled and did his best to mollify the deeply insulted ambassador. On 12 August he wrote to the Privy

Council demanding to know what on earth the Master of the Revels had thought he was doing to sanction the performance of such a piece and requiring them to summon the King's Men and the writer before them immediately to demand an explanation. Therefore on the tenth day of what had been described as 'the nine days' wonder', the Globe was closed, the King's Men banned from acting and, a day later, a summons issued for the arrest of Middleton.

On 18 August the King's Men, less Middleton, appeared before the Privy Council arraigned on the grounds that it was forbidden to represent any contemporary Christian king on stage, as they must have well known, and that it had been obvious who the White and Black chess kings were supposed to represent. They were fortunate that they were not gaoled but discharged with 'a round and sharp reproof', forbidden to act again until the King's pleasure was known, and bound over to the tune of £300. In their defence the King's Men, so the Privy Council informed the King on 21 August, 'had produced a book, being an original and perfect copy thereof (or so they affirmed) as seen and allowed by Sir Henry Herbert, Knight, Master of the Revels, under his own hand and subscribed by him in the last page of the said book'. It had also been made clear to the unfortunate Sir Henry that he was scarcely fit to hold his office, though presumably the script had gone through on the nod among a number of others.

On first receiving the summons for his arrest 'by Royal decree', Middleton at first simply refused to obey it. The Council duly reported the situation to His Majesty, that 'one Middleton, who, shifting out of the way and not attending the Board as was expected, we have given the warrant for the apprehending of him'. Finally on 27 August, after scouring London for him without success, a further warrant was issued, this time for the arrest of his son, Edward, in an attempt to ensure his father's compliance. It did and three days later Middleton gave himself up. A tradition preserved in a contemporary hand-written note in a manuscript of the play, which belonged to a man called Dyson, records that 'Middleton was committed to prison where he lay for some good time and at last got out upon a Petition to the King'.

Eventually the political crisis died down. After a while the actors were allowed to return to the Globe and perform again and Middleton was released from gaol to continue his joint employment as a freelance dramatist and as the official City Chronologer, to which position he had been appointed in 1620 at a salary of £6 13*s* 4*d*, increased a year later to £10. He certainly had to earn his money, for the holder of the office had to keep a journal of City events, write speeches for the Lord Mayor and senior Aldermen, and devise 'entertainments' when requested to do so. He appears to have carried out his tasks conscientiously – which is more than can be said for Ben Jonson who succeeded him in the position. He found the money came in handy but did as little to earn it as he possibly could.

FOURTEEN

Exit Ben Jonson

When I a verse shall make,
Know I have prayed thee
For old religion's sake,
Saint Ben to aid me.
Candles I'll give to thee
And a new altar;
And thou Saint Ben, shalt be
Writ in my psalter.

Robert Herrick, *Jonson Verbius* (1638)

During the winter of 1624–5 the King's Men suffered a further blow with the death of their house dramatist, John Fletcher. Some sources say he was a victim of the plague since it was virulent once again during the winter of 1624–5, or possibly because of Aubrey's reference to it:

John Fletcher, invited to go with a Knight of Norfolk or Suffolk in the Plague time of 1625, stayed to make himself a suit of clothes, and while it was making fell sick of the Plague and died. This I had from his tailor who is now a very old man, and the clerk of St. Mary Overy's in Southwark. Mr. Fletcher had an issue on his arm. The clerk (who was wont to bring him leaves to dress it), when he came found the spots upon him. Death stopped his journey and laid him low here.[1]

What militates against the supposition is that Fletcher received separate burial in a church rather than being thrown into a plague pit with the rest of the victims, among whom, quite possibly, was William Rowley who died at about the same time.

But outside the narrow confines of their own world, theatrical deaths passed largely unremarked and 1625 saw a far more important demise, that of King James. The accession of his son, Charles I, was to usher in a very different kind of Court with very different tastes and interests. The new King made it clear from the start that he would not tolerate slovenliness in dress or rude or drunken behaviour from anyone. His was to be a Court of elegant sobriety and those who presented themselves before him the worse for drink received short shrift, as did those free with 'sordid words'. He enjoyed theatrical entertainment but of a tasteful kind.

In 1626 Edward Alleyn died, releasing his young wife, John Donne's daughter Constance, from what for her had been a deeply unsatisfactory marriage and leaving behind the enormous sum of £10,000 to endow his college. He, in turn, was followed a year later by Middleton who died at his home in Newington Butts and was buried in the parish churchyard on 4 July 1627. He died, as he had lived, in straitened circumstances and the following year his wife, Magdalen, was forced to appeal to the city fathers for financial help. She was granted twenty nobles.

During the next few years virtually all the surviving playwrights of the golden age were to follow. Chapman's last published work appeared in 1629 under the extraordinary title *A Justification of a Strange Action of Nero burying with a Solemn Funeral one of the Cast Hairs of his Mistress Poppaea; Also a Just reproof of a Roman smell-feast, being the fifth satire of the Juvenal translated*. History does not record whether or not it was a success but it hardly seems likely that it was a bestseller in such changed times. He died on 12 May 1634 and was buried in the churchyard of St Giles in the Fields in a tomb designed by his friend, Inigo Jones. Marston, who had resigned his living in 1631, died in June of the same year and was buried in the Temple Church, next to his father. We do not know what happened to Webster, even whether or not he married, except that by 1634 he was bracketed with Fletcher as a dead playwright; nor is there any record of what happened to Ford.

The demise of Philip Massinger, best known for his *A New Way to Pay Old Debts* which has received several recent revivals, offers a little mystery. His burial is registered as having taken place on 18 March 1638. He was living on the Bankside and was apparently in good health but 'went to bed well and was dead before morning', whereupon his body 'being accompanied by "comedians" [actors] was buried about the middle of the churchyard belonging to St. Saviour's Church'. He was said to have been buried in the same grave as his friend John Fletcher, but this is most unlikely if indeed Fletcher was a plague victim. The last we hear of Dekker is that he boasted he had reached the age of 'three score' and was still writing pamphlets in 1638.

Their deaths or disappearances provoked little or no comment. A whole generation of theatregoers had grown up since John Burbage first built The Theatre, many of whom would never even have heard of those early University Wits, or the fates which befell Kyd and Marlowe, except as dramatists whose work they enjoyed, nor would they be able to imagine a time before there were any playhouses. That first wave of dramatists, thrust suddenly into the public eye, the roaring boys of the 1590s with their determinedly outrageous behaviour, belonged to the past. Dramatists were no longer considered remarkable and anyway tastes had changed; city satires, Marlowe's 'mighty line', historical epics, wordy (and worthy) plays were now quite out of fashion. Elegant and amusing comedies and ever more elaborate masques were what people wanted to see, particularly the Court.

By the 1630s the most popular playwrights were James Shirley, Richard Brome (who had once been Jonson's servant) and the young William Davenant, who neither confirmed nor denied the strong rumour that he was Shakespeare's son, rather than his godson. Certainly Shakespeare had known his mother, Jennifer, when she lived in London and regularly stayed overnight at the inn later run by her and her husband in Oxford. Anyway such a piece of gossip was hardly likely to hinder the career of a would-be writer.

Shirley had first taken Holy Orders, gone on to become a Catholic, then transferred his interests to the theatre, writing tragedies, popular comedies and masques, always with an eye to what was fashionable and careful not to upset the authorities. He shamelessly plagiarised the works of others, although that was hardly unusual, even producing his own version of *The Duchess of Malfi* under the title of *The Cardinal*, but he was best known for his comedies like *The Gamester* and *Hyde Park*. Brome, however, possibly because of his close association with Jonson, brought with him more than a whiff of that older theatrical world, especially with *The Antipode*, in which a miserly, autocratic man is persuaded that he has been transported there and that in this new world everything is the opposite from that in the old: the poor rule the rich, women have the upper hand on men and masters wait on servants. He also has the doubtful privilege of having the last play, *The Jovial Crew*, to be given a London production before the Civil War. Davenant had some small success as a dramatist before the war but was to play a far more crucial role after it than that of a writer.

The last remaining major figure linking the age of Elizabeth to the present-day Court of King Charles I was Ben Jonson, now an increasingly isolated and unfashionable figure, although King James's gift of a state pension for life had made him, to all intents and purposes, England's first Poet Laureate. But his style of writing, particularly for the theatre, simply did not suit any more even when, as in *A Staple of News*, he chose a topical subject, mocking the new fashion for publishing 'newspapers', an innovation looked on by the authorities with increasing alarm. His account of its first night rings all too true to any playwright who even now finds him/herself hanging around helplessly backstage before so crucial a performance. He describes his fraying nerves, his trundling in and out of the 'tiring house' and dressing room to give his advice to the actors before going off to have yet another drink. Such last minute advice is never welcome and has never been encouraged, but Jonson's interference in productions was legendary, actors complaining that he prompted them loudly if they dried, railed at the bookholder (prompter), cursed the wardrobe master, shouted at the musicians and made them sweat for every last mistake they made.[2]

Snubbed by the new regime, he founded the Apollo Club, its headquarters in a Fleet Street tavern, where he could surround himself with congenial company. He drew up his own set of rules for it, one of which might be welcome now since it stated that there was no music to be played by 'a saucy fiddler presuming to intrude', unless the musician was actually invited to do so. Another, that women were allowed to attend meetings by invitation, is more than can be said of today's Garrick Club. In 1628 he suffered a severe stroke and was virtually bedridden for the rest of his life, describing himself as being 'blocked up and straitened [*sic*], narrowed in, fixed to the bed and boards, unlike to win health or scarce breath'. He wrote to King Charles, in elegant verse, asking for an increase in his pension, but his request was ignored. He was comforted in his last years by a coterie of young men, known as the Tribe of Ben, who admired him as a poet. In spite of his physical affliction the following year he managed one more play, *The New Inn*, which was performed by the King's Men at the Blackfriars Theatre, but it was not a success. He died in poverty on 6 August 1637 leaving behind a pile of unfinished manuscripts, an old wicker chair 'such as women use', and goods to the value of only £8 8*s* 6*d*. His estranged wife was long dead and there were no surviving children.

He did, however, achieve burial in Westminster Abbey, not in Poet's Corner with Chaucer and Beaumont, but in the north aisle. It is said that some time previously Jonson joked with the Dean of Westminster that he could not afford to be buried alongside the other poets as he was too big and it would cost too much. He suggested, therefore, that he should be buried standing up. This was considered apocryphal until the early nineteenth century, when a Lady Wilson came to be buried in the north aisle; Jonson's cheap coffin was there, standing on end. Carved on his stone are the simple words: 'O Rare Ben Jonson'.

His death finally drew a line under that extraordinary era which had witnessed not only the very beginnings of professional theatre but also its greatest ever flowering of dramatic writing talent. It not only produced the towering talent of Shakespeare but also offered

Marlowe, Ben Jonson and Thomas Middleton in the first rank, with Greene, Peele, Kyd, Dekker, Webster, Rowley, Marston, Chapman, Heywood, Massinger, Beaumont and Fletcher and Tourneur following close behind. It brought into being a whole new art form and a truly professional class of actors and writers, almost all of whom were drawn from modest backgrounds and who, thanks to a particular combination of circumstances, were offered creative fulfilment beyond their wildest dreams. It has never happened again.

In 1642 the curtain came down with the passing of the Edict stating that all stage performances were banned. It was a catastrophe for the players. For sixty years they had been licensed to perform. It had always been a hazardous profession, playhouses could be closed at short notice because of the plague, play-acting continued to be castigated by critics, they were at risk of offending the authorities even if it was unintentional and it was always a hand-to-mouth existence, but the professional theatre had survived it all. But the frantic pleas of actors and writers fell on deaf ears and after the end of hostilities, worse was to come. On 9 February 1648 a new Ordinance was enacted ordering the demolition of all the playhouses, the arrest of any actors found performing anywhere and substantial fines for each and every person found attending any kind of dramatic presentation. Indeed all forms of public entertainment were banned, even dancing round the maypole.

For eighteen years theatre went dark in England. Only towards the end of the Commonwealth was anyone brave enough to try again, and that person was William, now Sir William, Davenant. Having returned from France where he had been in exile with Prince Charles, he returned to London determined that one way or another he would bring back theatre and to this end set about ingratiating himself with Cromwell. He actually persuaded the Protector to allow him to write a little entertainment for his daughter's wedding, along with a patriotic piece geared to promote the government line on its relationship with Spain. It was a major breakthrough.

With the Restoration in sight, actors started to trickle back to London from exile either abroad or in the country and quietly start to rehearse. With the return of the King, theatre was back in business. But it was theatre of a very different kind. Charles II and his Court, used now to the continental way of doing things, demanded playhouses with the new 'picture frame' stage, distancing the audience from the actors and completely altering the English style of acting. Not only that, women were finally allowed on stage even if the general belief was that they were no better than they should be and only doing it to attract the attention of a wealthy keeper, an attitude reflected in the Restoration Comedies, amusing as many of them are. As for the rest, nobody wanted the old plays, not even those of Shakespeare. *Antony and Cleopatra* was supplanted by Dryden's *Love for Love* and until the time of Edmund Kean it was Colley Cibber's version of *Richard III* to which audiences flocked.

Adrian Noble, a previous artistic director of the Royal Shakespeare Company, says:

during the thirty-year period in which these plays were written, enormous political shifts were taking place. All that was reflected in the drama. The plays alert audiences' imagination and edify it, not in a smug way, but because they are truly big experiences, great epic public experiences and the greatest single experience of the age is Shakespeare where you can have a laugh, followed by a love scene, followed by a battle, followed by political intrigue in a council chamber, followed by a rough street scene and all within twenty minutes.

He might have added that this was possible because of the big open space which was the stage and also because the action was not held up in those early days by the trundling in of elaborate scenery on trucks or flying sets down from the roof. Parts of Shakespeare's *Antony and Cleopatra* read almost like a film or television script with scenes only a few lines long during which the action moves between Rome and Egypt. The audience would know which part of the stage represented each country and all an actor had to do was to walk across it. The speed added to the excitement.

Noble continues:

This is the thread which runs through all these plays and the measure of their continuing success in their impact on the public. What we see are big public issues debated in big public plays. They have the freedom of form because these playwrights virtually invented their own, even though they stole ideas from all over the place, but they were thieves who invented as they went along, saying to themselves 'I'll talk to the audience at this point', or 'I think I'll bring a ghost in here'. In terms of reality it didn't worry them at all because they were creating, play by play, their own worlds. The audiences would have applauded them at the end and then, quite possibly, gone off and cheered a public hanging![3]

It is impossible to surmise what the fate of the sixteenth and early seventeenth-century dramatists would have been had there not been a William Shakespeare, although it was not until nearly two hundred years after his death that he actually received the theatrical respect he deserved. But there is no doubt that so towering a talent totally overshadowed that of his contemporaries. Productions of their plays, other than Marlowe's *Dr. Faustus*, and Ben Jonson's *The Alchemist* and *Volpone*, were rarities until well into the middle of the twentieth century. The building of two new theatres, the Royal Shakespeare Company's Swan Theatre in Stratford-upon-Avon and the new Globe on the banks of the Thames, close to the site of the original, has happily changed the situation for the better and new audiences have laughed at Marston and Jonson's *Eastward Ho!*, Jonson's *The Devil's an Ass* and Middleton's *A Mad World My Masters*. Like their Elizabethan counterparts they have been thrilled and pleasantly horrified by Tourneur's *Revenger's Tragedy*, Middleton and Rowley's *The Changeling*, Webster's *Duchess of Malfi* and *White Devil*. Marlowe's *Tamburlaine* and *Edward II* have both had productions in recent years. While a proportion of the plays written to fill the playhouses were potboilers which have rightly sunk with little trace, there remains a large body of work on which to draw.

Perhaps we should leave the last word to 'I.C.', the anonymous author of *Two Merry Milkmaids* who, in his Prologue, wishes on his audience then what we hope they will find in that same body of work today:

We hope, for your own good, you in the yard
Will lend your ears, attentively to hear
Things that shall flow so smoothly to your ear,
That you returning to your friends shall say,
How e'er you understood it, 'T'was a fine Play'.

Notes

Although in some cases the author has worked from original documents, where possible publications in which they are more easily accessible are given as a source.

Introduction

1. A.D. Wright and V.F. Stern, *In Search of Christopher Marlowe* (Macdonald 1965), p. 137.

Chapter One

1. M.C. Bradbrook, *The Rise of the Common Player* (Cambridge University Press 1962), p. 52.
2. Ibid., pp. 56–67.
3. Ibid.
4. Ibid. (quoting Stephen Gosson's pamphlet of 1582), pp. 72–4.
5. Andrew Gurr, *The Elizabethan Stage* (Cambridge University Press 1980), pp. 113 ff.
6. *Henslowe's Diary*, ed. R.A. Roakes and R.T. Rickert (Cambridge University Press 1961), pp. 274–5.
7. Bradbrook, *Rise of the Common Player* (quoting from Stockwood's Sermon of 24 August 1587), p. 101.
8. Andrew Gurr, *Playgoing in Shakespeare's London* (Cambridge University Press 1987), pp. 206–7.

Chapter Two

1. Seminar on Elizabethan Theatre, Shakespeare Birthplace Trust, 2002.
2. *Fair Maid of the West* by Thomas Heywood (Methuen edn 1986), Act I Scene iii.

3. Robert Greene, *A Groatsworth of Wit Bought with a Million of Repentance* (pamphlet, Bodley Head Quartos, Vol. IV 1922).
4. Judith Cook, *Dr Simon Forman* (Chatto & Windus 2001), pp. 113–14.
5. *Privy Council Registers, Elizabeth I* (Public Record Office), vol. VI, P381b. This is published in many biographies of Marlowe, including Wraight and Stern, *Marlowe*, p. 88, along with a facsimile of the original.
6. S. Schoenbaum, *Shakespeare, A Documentary Life* (complete edn, Oxford University Press 1970), indexed under Katherine Hamlet.
7. Mark Eccles, *Shakespeare in Warwickshire* (University of Winsconsin Press 1963), p. 82.

Chapter Three

1. Andrew Gurr, *Shakespearean Stage*, p. 88.
2. *Henslowe's Diary*, pp. 38–40.
3. *The Works of Thomas Nashe*, ed. R.B. McKerrow, revised F.P. Wilson (Oxford University Press 1958), vol. III, pp. 311–12.
4. Bradbrook, *Rise of the Common Player*, pp. 74–5.
5. Ibid, quoting Northwood, pp. 69–70.

Chapter Four

1. *A Notable Discovery of Cosenage* and *The Art of Cony-Catching* (Bodley Head Quartos, Vol. 5, 1922). There are many editions of these pamphlets.
2. *A Gull's Horn Book* (facsimile edn, Scolar Press 1969).
3. Bradbrook, *Rise of the Common Player*, chapter note 13, p. 292.

Chapter Five

1. A.L. Rowse, *Christopher Marlowe* (Macmillan 1964), pp. 154–5.
2. A.L. Rowse, *William Shakespeare* (Macmillan 1965), pp. 124–5.
3. S. Schoenbaum, *Shakespeare, A Documentary Life* (Compact edn, Oxford University Press 1977), p. 205.
4. Jonathan Bate, *The Genius of Shakespeare* (Picador 1997), pp. 24–5 (and almost all other biographies).
5. Wraight and Stern, *Marlowe*, quoting from Middlesex Sessions Roll 284, Elizabeth I 1589, pp. 117–23.
6. R.B. McKerrow, *Works of Thomas Nashe*, Vol. III, p. 168.
7. Wraight and Stern, *Marlowe*, pp. 120–2.
8. *Henslowe's Diary*, pp. 276–7.
9. J. Cook, *Dr Simon Forman*, from Ashmol Folio 280.
10. F. Laroque, *Shakespeare, Court and Playhouse* (Thames & Hudson 1977), pp. 146–7, a useful small compendium of general information which includes the Chettle apology in full.

Chapter Six

1. Wraight and Stern, *Marlowe*, pp. 151 ff.
2. Ibid., pp. 235–7, quoting Dr S.A. Tannenbaum, *The Book of Sir Thomas More* (Tenny Press, New York), Chap. VII, p. 59.
3. Ibid.

4. *Henslowe's Diary*, p. 274.
5. Thomas Kyd, *Touching Marlowe's Monstrous Opinions*, British Library Mss Harley 6848 143 ff., 1593, also Charles Nicholls, *The Reckoning* (Jonathan Cape 1992), pp. 45–6. Alexis was in the original verse in Virgil's *Ecloques*.
6. J. Hotson, *The Death of Christopher Marlowe* (Harvard University Press 1925). This small, but vital, book gives details of the inquest and facsimile of part of the report of the proceedings. This was a breakthrough piece of research. For those interested there is a wealth of material, including F.S. Boas, *Christopher Marlowe, A Critical Study* (Oxford University Press 1940), Charles Norman, *The Muses' Darling* (Falcon Press 1947) and Nicholls, *The Reckoning*, as above.
7. Nicholls, *The Reckoning*, pp. 17–18 and 325–9.
8. 'The Baines Note', British Library Harley Mss 6853, 1593 pp. 307–8ff. (copy) also Wraight and Stern, *Marlowe*, text of note p. 302, facsimile 308–9.

Chapter Seven

1. Both petitions in full in *Henslowe's Diary*, pp. 284–5.
2. *Depositions of Witnesses before the Commission Held at Cerne Abbas in Dorset on 21 March 1594 in answer to Interrogatories concerning Atheism and Apostasy*, British Library Harley Mss 6848, pp. 183–90 ff.
3. John Aubrey, *Brief Lives* (Penguin English Library 1972), pp. 128–9.
4. *Henslowe's Diary*, p. 286.

Chapter Eight

1. Gurr, *Playgoing in Shakespeare's London* (quoting Stubbs, *The Anatomy of Abuses*), p. 40.

2. Gurr, as above (quoting Henry Peacham, *The Art of Living in London*, 1622 edn), p. 6.
3. Bradbrook, *Rise of the Common Player*, p. 101.
4. Cook, *Dr Simon Forman*, pp. 309–11 (quoting from *Book of Plaies and Notes Thereof Per Forman* (Bodleian Library, Ashmol Folio 208).
5. Sonnet 74, Gurr, *Playgoing in Shakespeare's London*, p. 215.
6. *Taylor's Revenge, or the Rymer William Fennor firkt, ferrited and finely fecht over the Coals.* Taylor's papers are chaotic. The account is contained in *The Works of John Taylor the Water Poet* published in 1630. The copy used is in Gloucester Library, where it is pointed out that there are errors in pagination, missing pages and pages without numbers, of which this is one.
7. Gurr, *Playgoing in Shakespeare's London* (quoting Sir John Davies *In Cosmum*), p. 66.

Chapter Nine

1. Gurr, *Playgoing in Shakespeare's London*, p. 66.
2. *Shakespeare in the Public Records*, compiled by David Thomas (Her Majesty's Stationery Office 1985), pp. 22–3, including facsimile of relevant document.
3. Rowse, *William Shakespeare*, pp. 279–80.
4. *Henslowe's Diary*, p. 125.
5. There are many accounts of the Poets' War on which this chapter is based including Anne Barton, *Ben Jonson, Dramatist* (Cambridge University Press 1984), all Chapter 3, and Marchette Chute, *Ben Jonson of Westminster* (Robert Hale 1954), pp. 109–11; also J. Cook, *At the Sign of the Swan* (Harrap 1986), pp. 92–4.

Chapter Ten

1. Quotations taken from the programme notes for the production of Middleton's *Women Beware Women* by the RSC in 1970. The programme contains much useful information and a copy is available in the Shakespeare Birthplace Trust Library, Stratford-upon-Avon.
2. For argument, see Martin and White, *Middleton and Tourneur* (Macmillan 1992).
3. Barton, *Ben Jonson, Dramatist*, pp. 92–105.
4. *Ben Jonson's Conversations with William Drummond of Hawthornden* (published by the Shakespeare Society, 1842).
5. *Elizabethan and Jacobean Comedies* edited by Brian Gibbons (New Mermaid edn, Ernest Benn Ltd 1984), appendix B.

Chapter Eleven

1. We have the late Dr A.L. Rowse to thank for bringing Emilia into the light of day, albeit with much controversy since he was convinced she was the Dark Lady of the Sonnets. Information on her can be found in *Ashmol Folios* 226 and 354, Rowse, *The Casebooks of Simon Forman* (Picador 1976), pp. 100–28 and *The Poems of Shakespeare's Dark Lady* (Macmillan 1978).
2. *The Life and Death of Mistress Mary Frith*, anonymous pamphlet published 1616. G. Salgarado, *The Elizabethan Underworld* (Alan Sutton 1977), pp. 22–3 and 42–4, J. Cook, *At the Sign of the Swan*, pp. 151–5.
3. Thomas Middleton and Thomas Dekker, *The Roaring Girl*, III, i.

Chapter Twelve

1. Richard Huggett, *The Curse of Macbeth* (Huggett & Picton 1981), p. 144.
2. Aubrey, *Brief Lives*, p. 252.
3. Robert Speaight, *Shakespeare,The Man and his Achievements* (Dent 1977), p. 140 (and many other biographies).
4. J. Cook, *Shakespeare's Players* (Harrap 1983), pp. 24–5.
5. M.C. Bradbrook, *John Webster, Citizen and Dramatist* (Weidenfeld & Nicolson 1980), p. 41.
6. Ibid., p. 169.
7. Gurr, *Playgoing in Shakespeare's London*, appendix 2, pp. 226–7.
8. Schoenbaum, *A Documentary Life* (compact edition), p. 252.
9. Speaight, *Shakespeare, the Man and his Achievements*, p. 371 (and in virtually all biographies of Shakespeare).

Chapter Thirteen

1. Gurr, *Playgoing in Shakespeare's London*, appendix 2, p. 233.
2. Jonson's *Conversations with William Drummond*.
3. Ibid.
4. Introduction to Thomas Middleton's *A Game At Chess*, ed. J.W. Harper (New Mermaid edn), pp. xii–xxiv. Also White, *Middleton and Tourneur*, Chapter 9.

Chapter Fourteen

1. Aubrey, *Brief Lives*, p. 129.
2. Chute, *Ben Jonson of Westminster*, pp. 296–7.
3. Conversation with author.

Bibliography

Books are published in London unless otherwise stated.

Manuscripts

Bodleian Library, Oxford, Ashmol Mss, Forman Papers ff. 208, 226, 280, 354
British Library, Harley Mss 6846 ff. 143
British Library, Harley Mss 6848 ff. 183–90
British Library, Harley Mss 6853 ff. 307/308 (The 'Baines' Note)
British Library, Roxburgh Collection, *Complaint and Lamentation of Mistress Arden of Faversham in Kent*, 1630, vol. III
Public Record Office, Privy Council Registers, Elizabeth I, vol. VI, p. 381

Published Papers, etc.

The Shakespeare Apocrypha, Oxford University Press, Oxford 1908
The Shakespeare Documents, vols I and II, ed. B. Roland Lewis, Oxford University Press, Oxford 1940
Shakespeare in the Public Records, compiled by David Thomas, Her Majesty's Stationery Office,1985
Shakespeare, A Documentary Life, S. Shoenbaum, Oxford University Press, Oxford, Complete Edition 1970, 'Compact Edition' 1977
Ben Jonson's Conversations with William Drummond of Hawthornden (Shakespeare Society 1842)
The Life and Death of Mistress Mary Frith (anonymous pamphlet 1616)

Books

Abbreviations: OUP, Oxford University Press. CUP, Cambridge University Press.

Adams, J.Q. *The Dramatic Records of Sir Henry Tylney*, New Haven, USA, 1917
Aubrey, J. *Brief Lives*, Penguin English Library, 1972
Bakeless, J. *Christopher Marlowe*, Harvard University Press, 1942
Barton, A. *Ben Jonson, Dramatist*, Cambridge, CUP, 1984
Bate, J. *The Genius of Shakespeare*, Picador, 1997
Bentley, G. *The Jacobean and Caroline Stage*, Oxford, OUP, 1941
Black, J.B. *The Reign of Elizabeth*, Oxford, OUP, 1959
Boas, F.S. *Christopher Marlowe*, Oxford, OUP, 1940
Bowsher, J. *The Rose Theatre*, London Museum Press, 1998
Bradbrook, J.B. *The Rise of the Common Player*, Cambridge, CUP, 1962
——. *John Webster*, Weidenfeld & Nicolson, 1980
Chambers, E.K. *The Elizabethan Stage*, Oxford, OUP, 1923

Bibliography

——. *Shakespeare – A Study of Facts and Problems*, OUP, 1989
Chute, M. *Ben Jonson of Westminster*, Robert Hale, 1954
Cook, J. *Shakespeare's Players*, Harrap, 1983
——. *At the Sign of the Swan*, Harrap, 1986
——. *Dr. Simon Forman – A Most Notorious Physician*, Chatto & Windus, 2001
Dekker, T. *A Gull's Horn Book*, Scolar Press edn, 1969
Dunn, T.A. *Philip Massinger*, London, 1957
Eccles, M. *Shakespeare in Warwickshire*, University of Winsconsin Press, 1963
Ellis-Fermor, U. *The Jacobean Drama*, London, 1936
Foakes, R.A. and Rickert, T.R. (eds) *Henslowe's Diary*, Cambridge, CUP, 1961
Freeman, A. *Thomas Kyd, Facts and Problems*, London, 1967
Fripp, E. *Shakespeare's Stratford*, Oxford, OUP, 1928
Greene, R. *A Notable Discovery of Cosenage and A Groatsworth of Wit Bought with a Million of Repentance*, Bodley Head Quartos Vol. IV 1922, Vol. V 1932
Gurr, A. *The Shakespearean Stage 1574–1642*, Cambridge, CUP, 1980
——. *Playgoing in Shakespeare's London*, Cambridge, CUP, 1987
Hosking, G.L. *The Life and Times of Edward Alleyn*, London, 1952
Hotson, J.L. *The Death of Christopher Marlowe*, Harvard University Press, 1926
Hugget, R. *The Curse of Macbeth*, Huggett & Picton, 1981
Jenkins, E. *Elizabeth the Great*, Gollancz, 1958
Knights, L.C. *Drama and Society in the Age of Jonson*, London, 1937
Laroque, F. *Shakespeare, Court, Crowd and Playhouse*, Thames & Hudson, 1977
McKerrow. R.B. (ed.) *The Works of Thomas Nashe*, vol. III. Oxford, OUP, 1958
Morris, B. *John Webster*, London, 1972
Mulryne, J.R. *Thomas Middleton*, London, 1979
Nicholl, C. *A Cup of News*, Routledge & Kegan Paul, 1984
——. *The Reckoning*, Picador, 1993
Nicoll, A. *Essays on Shakespeare and Elizabethan Drama*, University of Missouri Press, 1962
Ordish, T.F. *Early Elizabethan Theatres*, White Lion Press, 1894, revised 1971
Porter, L. (general ed.) *The Revels History of Drama: Vol III 1576–1613*, Methuen 1975, *Vol. IV 1613–1660*, 1980
Prouty, C.T. *Life and Works of George Peele*, Yale University Press, 1952
Rowse, A.L. *The England of Elizabeth*, Macmillan, 1950
——. *Christopher Marlowe*, Macmillan, 1962
——. *William Shakespeare*, Macmillan, 1964
——. *The Casebooks of Simon Forman*, Weidenfeld & Nicolson, 1974
——. *The Poems of Shakespeare's Dark Lady*, Macmillan, 1978
Rowse, A.L. and Harrison G.B., *Queen Elizabeth and Her Subjects*, Allen & Unwin, 1935
Salgado, G. *The Elizabethan Underworld*, Stroud, Alan Sutton, 1971
Seccombe and Allen, *The Age of Shakespeare*, London, 1903
Speaight, R. *Shakespeare, the Man and his Achievements*, J.M. Dent, 1977
Wallis, L.B. *Beaumont and Fletcher*, Oxford, OUP, 1947
White, M. *Middleton and Tourneur*, Cambridge, CUP, 1992
Wraight, A.D. and Stern, V.C. *In Search of Christopher Marlowe*, Macdonald, 1965
Young, J. *Penguin Social History of Britain – The Sixteenth Century*, 1984

Useful Play Scripts

A Game At Chess, Middleton, ed. J.W. New, Mermaids, Ernest Benn, 1966

Elizabethan and Jacobean Comedies, ed. Brian Gibbons, Ernest Benn, 1984

Fair Maid of the West, Heywood, ed. Keith Sturgess, Methuen, 1986

Four Tudor Comedies, ed. William Tydeman, Penguin English Library, 1984

Six Plays by Contemporaries of Shakespeare, ed. C.B. Wheeler, OUP, 1971

The Devil's an Ass, Jonson, Nick Hern Books, 1995

The Roaring Girl, ed. Havelock Ellis, Mermaid Old Masters edition, 1890

The Witch of Edmonton, Dekker, Ford, Rowley, Methuen, 1983

Three Elizabethan Domestic Tragedies, ed. K. Sturgess, Penguin Classics, 1969

Three Jacobean Tragedies, ed. G. Salgado, Penguin English Library, 1965

Subheadings are arranged in ascending order of the first page number.

Index